★ ★ ★ ★ ★ ★ ★ ★ ★ ★

AMERICAN
DREAM

 ★ ★ ★ ★ ★ ★ ★

FRANK A. THOMAS

A Christian Way Out
of the Great Recession

Abingdon Press
Nashville

American Dream 2.0
A Christian Way Out of the Great Recession

Library of Congress Cataloging-in-Publication Data

Thomas, Frank A. (Frank Anthony), 1955–
  American dream 2.0 : a Christian way out of the great recession / Frank A. Thomas.
     p. cm.
  ISBN 978-1-4267-5390-9 (book - pbk. / trade pbk. : alk. paper) 1. Jeremiads—United States.
2. Christianity and politics—United States. 3. African Americans—History. 4. African Americans—Religion. 5. Recessions—United States. I. Title.
  BR516.T46 2012
  261.0973—dc23

                                                                                        2012008013

Unless otherwise indicated, all Scripture quotations are from the Common English Bible New Testament. Copyright © 2010 by the Common English Bible. All rights reserved. Used by permission. (www.CommonEnglishBible.com)

Scripture quotations marked MESSAGE are from *THE MESSAGE.* Copyright © by Eugene H. Peterson 1993, 1994, 1995, 1996, 2000, 2001, 2002. Used by permission of NavPress Publishing Group.

Excerpts from "Beyond Vietnam" are reprinted by arrangement with The Heirs to the Estate of Martin Luther King Jr., c/o Writers House as agent for the proprietor New York, NY.

Copyright 1967 Dr. Martin Luther King Jr; copyright renewed 1995 Coretta Scott King.

"Let America Be America Again" from THE COLLECTED POEMS OF LANGSTON HUGHES by Langston Hughes, edited by Arnold Rampersad with David Roessel, Associate Editor, copyright © 1994 by the Estate of Langston Hughes. Used by permission of Alfred A. Knopf, a division of Random House, Inc.

Epic of America excerpts are from EPIC OF AMERICA by James Truslow Adams. Copyright © 1932 by James Trunslow Adams. By permission of Little, Brown and Company. All rights reserved.

James Truslow Papers, 1918–1949, Rare Book & Manuscript Library, Columbia University in the City of New York.

Extracts from *The Speech: Race and Barack Obama's "A More Perfect Union"* are copyright © 2009, T. Denean Sharpley-Whiting, *The Speech: Race and Barack Obama's "A More Perfect Union,"* Bloomsbury USA.

Bob Cox, "Workers at Bankrupt American Airlines Say Do Not Blame Us: Wall Street Tied Bankruptcy to Labor Cost, but American's Top Brass Made Own Mistakes," January 5, 2012, reprinted by permission of the *Fort Worth Star-Telegram.*

Sacvan Bercovitch, "Investigations of an Americanist," *The Journal of American History* 78, no. 3 (December 1991), appears by permission of Oxford University Press.

To the memory of Michael Charles Leff,
dearly departed Chair of the Department of Communication
at the University of Memphis, professor, rhetorical scholar of the
highest order, teacher, mentor, dissertation adviser, and
most of all friend—without whose wisdom, guidance, and
unwavering support many of these insights would have lain dormant

CONTENTS

ACKNOWLEDGMENTS ix

INTRODUCTION xi

SECTION ONE:
THE RISE AND FALL OF THE AMERICAN DREAM 1
   1. The American Jeremiad and the Cultural Myth
      of America. 3
   2. The Cultural Myth of America 15
   3. The Fall of the American Dream 27

SECTION TWO:
PROPHETIC POLITICS AND THE AMERICAN DREAM 37
   4. Prophetic Reformation: Martin Luther King, Jr., and the
      Triumphant March to the American Dream 43
   5. Prophetic Transformation: Martin Luther King, Jr.,
      and "Beyond Vietnam" 51
   6. Prophetic Transformation: Jeremiah A. Wright, Jr., and
      the American Dream. 71
   7. Barack Obama and the Multicultural
      American Dream. 91

SECTION THREE:
THE BELOVED COMMUNITY 115
   8. The Rise of Capitalist Values 123
   9. The Beloved Community 131
  10. The Reign of God 149

EPILOGUE: ENCOURAGING THE
   CITIZEN-ACTIVIST 167

Contents

Discussion Guide 171
Notes 201

ACKNOWLEDGMENTS

Special thanks to Len Wilson for taking interest in the manuscript. I truly believe that the difference between a manuscript in the files and a manuscript being published is a really good editor. Thanks for making such a big difference. Thanks to the entire team at Abingdon Press. You have been wonderful to work with.

Special thanks to the Communication Department at the University of Memphis, especially retired professor John A. Campbell, M. Allison Graham, Katherine G. Hendrix, Antonio Raul deVelasco, Sandra Sarkela, and Amanda Young; Brad McAdon of the English Department; and my classmates Andre Johnson, Jill Greenman, and Mark Vail.

Special thanks to my family: my wife, Joyce, of thirty-five years, my son, Tony, and my daughter, Rachel, for patience and encouragement every step of the way while Daddy was "researching and writing, again."

Special thanks to my mother and father, John and Almetha Thomas, and my sister, Angela Edwards, and Frederick Thomas.

Special thanks to the family of Mississippi Boulevard Christian Church of Memphis, Tennessee, where I have the honor to serve as senior pastor. Special thanks to a wonderful staff and lay leadership team and an awesome executive assistant, Vera Banks.

Most of all, I thank God for the privilege of the ministry of the gospel of Jesus Christ.

INTRODUCTION

O, let America be America again—
The land that never has been yet—
And yet must be—
The land where every man is free.
The land that's mine—
The poor man's, Indian's, Negro's, ME—
Who made America,
Whose sweat and blood, whose faith and pain,
Whose hand at the foundry, whose plow in the rain,
Must bring back our mighty dream again.
—Langston Hughes

The term *American Dream* is only eighty years old. In the grim and turbulent atmosphere of the Great Depression in 1931, historian James Trunslow Adams published *The Epic of America* and coined the American Dream as:

> a better, richer, and happier life for all our citizens of every rank, which is the greatest contribution we have made to the thought and welfare of the world. That dream or hope has been present from the start. Ever since we became an independent nation, each generation has seen an uprising of ordinary Americans to save the American Dream from the forces which appear to be overwhelming it.[1]

Adams's words, true in 1931, are still true today; there is the need for "an uprising of ordinary Americans to save the American Dream." In the aftermath of the Great Recession, the worst economic downturn since the Great Depression, and the corresponding anemic and slow recovery, there are forces seeking to overwhelm the American Dream. There is persistent anxiety and vociferous questioning as to whether the American nation can deliver "a better, richer, and happier life for all our citizens of every rank." *Time* magazine recently ran the cover story "How to Restore the American Dream."[2] Countless magazine articles, academic essays, citizen blogs, newspaper editorials, and popular books all offer commentary on the American Dream and its relevance and meaning in contemporary America.[3]

Dating back to the mid-1980s, there has been a sense that the American Dream is slipping away or beyond reach of the average citizen. Given the recent near-collapse of our economic system; the taxpayer/government bailout of financial institutions thought heretofore to be virtually invincible; the painfully high unemployment and the persistent jobless recovery; that one quarter of American homes are "underwater," such that people owe more than their home is worth; the expansive and expanding economic gap among the rich, middle, and permanent underclass; the inability of the political system to offer relevant solutions; the nagging effects of globalization; and the increasing sense that the nation is moving in the wrong direction, there is a hue and cry across the land as to whether the American Dream can deliver "a better, richer, and happier life for all our citizens of every rank." Some have even concluded that the American Dream is dead.

Maybe the challenge is in reevaluating what has become the conventional wisdom and interpretation of the American Dream itself. The American Dream in its origin was conceived of as a ritual of benefit for a certain class of people, and not "every rank" within American society. Though our patriotic rhetoric touted America as being for "all," the reality was, and still is, that only certain groups and classes have access to the American Dream. Based upon the most recent numbers comparing the increase of wealth and income of a small number of Americans at the very top to the rest of the nation suffering unemployment, wage stagnation, and standard of living decline, many conclude that for the last thirty years only the rich have had access to the American Dream. Recognizing the vast economic and racial disparity in America,

Langston Hughes wrote of the deep yearning in the hearts of many who have not had access to the American Dream: "O, let America be America again . . . The land where every man is free. The land that's mine—the poor man's, Indian's, Negro's, ME—who made America."

Periodically in American history, corrective movements such as the civil rights movement of the mid-1950s to 1960s have attempted to expand the American Dream to wider and broader segments of America. But the ability of the American Dream to expand in its current conceptualization is fundamentally flawed. The American Dream has come to be exclusively defined from a materialistic perspective, with economic benefit its chief aim and the primary measure of human happiness. When we define the American Dream singularly in terms of economic benefit, a better, richer, and happier life for all is not possible without domination and exploitation of subjected people. What we need is a reconceptualization of the American Dream, to, in the words of Langston Hughes, "bring back our mighty dream again."

In light of wide-scale concerns about the uncertainty of the American Dream, what is the response of the American Christian church? Historically, the American church has had four primary responses. The first is to deny the truth and validity of the American Dream and, as a follower of Jesus Christ, embrace an ascetic form of discipleship. In this response, the disciple pulls away from the values of the culture into Christian community that offers true meaning and value in life. The second response is to completely support and endorse the American Dream through avowed patriotism, often comingling the Bible and the American flag. This true believer advocates American exceptionalism and promotes America's destiny as the greatest nation on earth and God's light of the world. The third response is to embrace some form of prosperity gospel, which is, in effect, the church's support of the rags-to-riches, Horatio Alger cultural myth, in which anyone can prosper and become a millionaire. In this response, America, like nowhere else on earth, is the land of opportunity. Prosperity gospel is a message of wealth and success, in which people change their individual consciousness in order to take advantage of vast and unlimited opportunity. The final response, and the thesis of this book, is the church as transformer or corrector of a flawed American culture. The church does not deny and pull away or uncritically endorse patriotism and prosperity gospel, but offers a prophetic critique of the American Dream and seeks to move the American Dream and a flawed culture into alignment with the values of the reign of God. This is social gospel that seeks to engage and transform culture, hence the title, *American Dream 2.0: A Christian Way Out of the Great Recession.* America needs an upgraded version of the American Dream that will move us beyond the values that resulted in the Great Recession.

The purpose of this book is to cause an uprising of ordinary American citizens—particularly pastors, their congregations, and all people of goodwill—to reclaim the American Dream from its exclusively economic stranglehold on the nation. Our challenge is to redevelop America without the exploitation or domination of subjected people. This America will look more like what Jesus would call the "reign of God" or what Martin Luther King, Jr., might call "the Beloved Community."

American Dream 2.0: A Christian Way Out of the Great Recession requires three major sections with corresponding chapters in each. The first section explores the rise and fall of the American Dream as the primary cultural myth of America. The second section demonstrates that the key to the fulfillment, expansion, and reclamation of the American Dream lies in the protest discourse of subjugated people for whom the American Dream was unfulfilled, or whom I call "prophets of the American Dream." The third section explores the implications of Martin Luther King, Jr.'s concept of the Beloved Community as a vision releasing the genius of America without the domination and subjugation of people. While modeled on Jesus' concept of the reign of God, King challenges American exceptionalism and offers practical insights that will help the reader reclaim the American Dream in this critical hour of our national life. In the final pages, I have included a workbook for the "citizen-activist" who might want to discover and implement specific strategies to bring about the Beloved Community. The workbook is designed for prayer, reflection, study, and action to bring about the reign of God.

In these hours of national turbulence similar to the upheavals of the Great Depression of the 1930s, we find the wonderful opportunity to reclaim America and make America what America should be. I am encouraged by Eugene Peterson's translation of Matthew 5:3, "You are blessed when you are at the end of your rope. With less of you, there is more of God and God's rule."[4] America is at the end of its rope, and I write this so that there will be more of God and God's rule.

Frank A. Thomas
April, 2012
Memphis, Tennessee

THE RISE AND FALL OF THE AMERICAN DREAM

THE AMERICAN JEREMIAD AND THE CULTURAL MYTH OF AMERICA

> *When He shall make us a praise and glory that men shall say of succeeding planta-*
> *tions, "May the Lord make it like that of New England." For we must consider that we*
> *shall be as a city upon a hill. The eyes of all people are upon us. So that if we shall deal*
> *falsely with our God in this work we have undertaken, and so cause Him to withdraw*
> *His present help from us, we shall be made a story and a by-word through the world.*
>   *—John Winthrop, "A Model of Christian Charity" (1630)*

The roots of the American Dream begin with the American jeremiad. The American jeremiad is:

> a mode of public exhortation that originated in the European
> pulpit, was transformed in both form and content by the New
> England Puritans, persisted through the eighteenth century, and
> helped sustain a national dream through two hundred years of
> turbulence and change.[1]

The American jeremiad gives shape and contour to the cultural myth and identity of America and, consistent with its early Puritan roots, establishes American values and ideals that are the basis of traditional and contemporary American life and community.

3

When I suggest the term *cultural myth,* I mean stories, legends, or explanations from the worldview of a particular people that serve to explain practices, beliefs, historical events, and even natural phenomena. For example, the legends of Greek gods such as Zeus, Apollo, and Pandora embodied the central ideas and values of Greek civilization. My interest is not to debate whether the stories are "true" in the literal sense. These myths functioned as key indicators of Greek cultural belief. They

> assured the Greeks of the nobility of their origins; they provided models for the roles Greeks would play in their public and private lives; they justified inequality in Greek society; they helped the Greeks understand human life and destiny in terms that "made sense" within the framework of that culture.[2]

Greek cultural myth functions the exact same way as American cultural myth. The cultural myths of America give Americans a "centrality," a shared way of looking at the world, an awareness of customs, values, habits, ideas, and beliefs, and a common language and vocabulary. Culture binds Americans together by shaping American tastes, habits, dreams, and desires. In fact, when we say *America,* we mean the bundle of American cultural myths that form the idea, identity, and place that the world has come to know as "America."

In this chapter, I briefly illustrate how the American jeremiad gives shape to the cultural myth of America. I will clarify the American jeremiad, from its Puritan parentage to its adoption by the African American community and from its theological roots to its secular dimensions in the formation of civil religion, including its enduring use in American and presidential politics. The American jeremiad also fosters a tradition of American dissent and establishes clear boundaries for any dissent that is a threat to American values and identity. I want to look first at the roots of the American jeremiad.

The European Jeremiad

In the eighth century B.C.E., the Judean prophet Isaiah spoke these words:

My loved one had a vineyard
  on a fertile hillside.
He dug it,
  cleared away its stones,
    planted it with excellent vines. . . .
He expected it to grow good grapes—
  but it grew rotten grapes.
So now, you who live in Jerusalem,
  you people of Judah,
    judge between me and my vineyard. . . .
Now let me tell you
  what I'm doing to my vineyard.
I'm removing its hedge,
  so it will be destroyed.
I'm breaking down its walls,
  so it will be trampled. . . .
The vineyard of
  the LORD of heavenly forces
  is the house of Israel,
  and the people of Judah. (Isaiah 5:1-7)

Isaiah's complaint, consistent with the prophecy of Jeremiah and that of other Hebrew prophets, functions to call the nation of Israel back to its covenant relationship with Yahweh. This passage, indicative of a love relationship between God and Israel, trumpets dire warnings of calamities and destruction by the prophets based upon Israel's sin and disobedience. Many of the Old Testament prophets bemoan Israel's idolatry and apostasy and utilize judgment and destruction as the basis for the call to repentance and a return to God's favor.

Drawing on sermons from the medieval pulpit and fifteenth- and sixteenth-century England, Europeans adopted the prophetic words of Isaiah and Jeremiah and of other prophets as a form of political sermon called the jeremiad. In its origins, a jeremiad was a lamentation or doleful complaint. It was a lament over the sins of the people based upon their departure from God's ways, and it warned of God's certain judgment and wrath to follow.

5

During the 1630s, New England Puritans interpreted the judgment of the European jeremiad as indicative of God's irrevocable wrath, and therefore, the inevitable, certain, and soon coming destruction of Europe. They believed that judgment was upon Europe, and based upon their covenant relationship with God, God had given America to them as the "new promised land." These seventeenth-century New England Puritans identified themselves as the "New Israel" and the "chosen people of God." Europe had forfeited its right to chosen-nation status, and many Puritans were fleeing to America to escape the upcoming and literal destruction of Europe. Upon their arrival, America was to be a "city set upon a hill." And when America strayed from the covenant, the American jeremiad was constructed to speak the judgment of God and call the people back to covenant with God.

The American Jeremiad

The American jeremiad was a public ritual designed to join social criticism to spiritual renewal, intertwining practical spiritual guidance with advice on public affairs. The jeremiad was the "state-of-the-covenant address, tendered at every public occasion (on days of fasting and prayer, humiliation and thanksgiving, at covenant renewal and artillery company ceremonies, and most elaborately and solemnly, at Election Day gatherings) observed by the Puritan colonist."[3]

The Puritan jeremiad reminded America of its divine mission established by John Winthrop in 1630. Winthrop, in a sermon at sea aboard the *Arabella*, paraphrased Matthew 5:14 to crystallize New England's mission: "we must consider that we shall be as a city upon a hill. The eyes of all people are upon us."[4] Given sacred history and a theocratic universe as the theatre for God's judgment, the Puritan migration to American was the "desacralization" of England and "the sacralization of the wilderness in America as a shelter and place for the Nonconformist Puritans."[5] The Puritans believed that their pilgrimage to America fulfilled prophetic apocalyptic and eschatological visions:

6

the Old and the New World were totally antagonistic and mutually exclusive entities. So, according to Puritan ideology of the migration to New England, the "discovery" of America was a great revelatory and prophetic event in the course of progress of the church upon the earth in which God's divine providence transformed the locus of the history of redemption and salvation from the corrupted Old World to the New World.[6]

Following this sense of divine mission, "the purpose of the jeremiads was to direct an imperiled people to God in order to fulfill their destiny, to guide them individually toward salvation, and collectively toward the American city of God."[7]

The unique feature of the American jeremiad was its unassailable optimism. In explicit opposition to the traditional European jeremiad, the American jeremiad inverts the doctrine of vengeance into a promise of ultimate success. The American jeremiad turned prophetic threat into celebration in that God's punishments were corrective and not ultimately destructive. There was no place in the American jeremiad for God's irrevocable wrath and the destruction of America in abandoning the covenant.

Unshakeable optimism is the essential characteristic of the American jeremiad. Any looming challenge is only a test of character and not a fatal error or structural flaw in the American system. Any crisis may be overcome by a return to the optimism of traditional American ideals rather than the identification of fundamental and structural flaws in American values. If there are concerns of subjugated groups over access to freedom, liberty, justice, citizenship, economic participation, equality, voting rights, and so on, it is a matter of unfulfilled values, that is, Americans not living up to their professed values, rather than fundamental and structural flaws in the nation.

Based in optimism rather than judgment, over a period of time, the American jeremiad provided a conceptual framework that defined and embraced acceptable dissent, or dissent that could gain a hearing in American culture. The result was that acceptable dissent functioned within the optimism of the American jeremiad and left fundamental and structural flaws in American values unchallenged.

The American Jeremiad and the
Cultural Myth of America

Shaped by the Puritans, the jeremiad, or the "political sermon," is a key rhetorical component in the shaping of the cultural myth of America. Puritan ideology shaped the cultural myth of America because it "represented the movement to modernity, and the myth they invented to express that aspects of their venture had provided the culture with a useful, flexible, durable and compelling fantasy of American identity."[8] In other words, Puritan theology and ideology shaped the idea that we have come to know as *America.* According to Sacvan Bercovitch, "the jeremiad is a central component in the development of America from colonies to nationhood and in the steady (if often violent) growth of middle-class culture."[9]

The War of 1812 solidified America's independence from Britain and contributed to an increased sense of nationhood. This increased sense of nationhood led to the establishment of the concept of *middle class,* when the term expresses "the norms we have come to associate with the free enterprise system," that is, hard work, frugality, individual initiative unhindered by government, and capitalistic economic striving.[10] The nation shifted from localized home production to large-scale manufacturing, and to maximize this change required not merely rivers and roads, but also canals and railroads to transfer raw materials and finished goods to increasingly distant farms, plantations, and towns of the Mississippi River Valley and cities that attracted immigrants. Despite financial depressions in 1819, 1837, and 1857, the middle class grew strong and vibrant.[11] M. Kathleen Kaveny, following Bercovitch, argues that "Calvinist values of hard work and frugality merged with the growth of capitalism to produce a 'middle-class' mindset of economic striving deemed to be both demanded and blessed by God himself."[12] These norms functioned as the officially endorsed cultural myth of America, and subsequently the American Dream. In its original Puritan version, the cultural myth of America was that America was a city set on a hill, blessed by God to be the light of the world, with the spiritual values of optimism, hard work, frugality, capitalistic economic striving, and a virgin land as assets to bring the kingdom of God to earth.

8

The myth of America became entrenched in New England and spread across the western territories and the South. The American Dream is a belief system and a way of life spun out in "webs of significance" by successive generations of Americans to justify their way of life to themselves and the world.[13] Despite its rootage in religion and the jeremiad, the American Dream assumed national and secular dimensions as American civil religion.

The Secular Form of the American Jeremiad

Based upon its establishment as part of American civil religion, the jeremiad has a quasi-religious secular form. David Howard-Pitney clearly illustrates the basic content of the argument of the jeremiad in its secular form:[14]

Premise 1: America has always believed itself to be special and uniquely set apart from the rest of the world, a shining example of socioreligious perfection lighting the way for the coming of God's kingdom.

Premise 2: American belief in the special role for America led to a "civil religion" replete with founding myths such as the pilgrims' arrival in America and the American Revolution, with patriarchs and saviors such as George Washington and Abraham Lincoln, and with holy Scriptures and sacred texts such as the Declaration of Independence and the Constitution.

Premise 3: Such a flattering self-image can promote both excessive social pride and complacency or an acute sense of failure in completing the transcendental mission. Therefore, the American jeremiad is the rhetoric of indignation, expressing deep dissatisfaction and urgently challenging the nation to reform.

Conclusion: The jeremiad expresses optimism, hope, and the conviction that the nation will reform and fulfill its special and unique destiny set apart from the rest of the world.[15]

The secular form of the jeremiad can be used by those of all political persuasions, including both Republicans and Democrats, liberals and conservatives. The secular jeremiadic form has been analyzed in speeches by Abraham Lincoln, Franklin D. Roosevelt, Richard Nixon, Jimmy Carter, Ronald Reagan, George W. Bush, and Barack Obama.[16] Kurt W. Ritter, studying the rhetoric of presidential nomination acceptance addresses, identifies the basic form of the secular jeremiad employed by many politicians:

> Each challenging candidate ultimately asks: "What made America great?" Posing this question allows the presidential aspirant to identify a single ideal (or a cluster of values) from our past which is missing in the present and whose absence accounts for our difficulties.[17]

Both the incumbent and the challenger identify from the ensemble of traditional American values, one or several ideals or values. Then, the incumbent or challenger explains what he or she has done or will do to keep America strong according to the chosen ideals within the set of traditional values. At the same time, the candidate draws sharp distinctions from his or her opponent by demonstrating how the opponent has strayed from the chosen traditional values and therefore has made or will make America weak. The candidate will then claim that no matter the crisis or difficulty America can return to its traditional greatness.

The classic example of the utilization of the secular jeremiad is the 1984 U.S. presidential campaign ad of Republican Party candidate Ronald Reagan, known as "Morning in America." The ad featured a montage of images of Americans going back to work and overcoming the difficulties of the late 1970s economy under then-president Jimmy Carter. A calm, optimistic narration suggested that it was morning again in America, based on the policies of Ronald Reagan's first term as president, and asked the question who would ever want to go back to the policies of the Democrats like his opponent, Walter Mondale, who had served as Carter's vice president. Reagan effectively employed the characteristic feature of the American jeremiad—its unassailable optimism. He adeptly illustrated that the economic crisis (caused and exacerbated by the opponent) was only a test of American character and not a fatal error or structural flaw in the American system. Despite the economic difficulties, it was morning in America. Many say that this optimism won the 1984 election, and has become, for some, the enduring legacy of Reagan's presidency.

With a preliminary understanding of the American jeremiad, let us turn now to consider the African American jeremiad.

African American Jeremiad

Although New England Puritans were the originators of the American jeremiad, African Americans quickly picked up the form to express their outrage at the sin of slavery. The African American jeremiad was primarily a northern-based free-black phenomenon because in the North it was relatively safe to protest openly against American slavery and racial proscription. Wilson Moses defines the black jeremiad as "constant warnings issued by blacks to whites, concerning the judgment that was to come from the sin of slavery":

> The black jeremiad was mainly a pre-Civil War phenomenon and showed the traditional preoccupation with impending doom. It was often directed at a white audience, and it bemoaned the sinfulness of slaveholders—fellow Americans who defied the natural and divine law that they were covenantally bound to uphold—and predicted God's punishment was to come. [18]

African Americans found the American jeremiad a natural form to express dissatisfaction with slavery and the general treatment of African Americans. [19]

In the two generations before the Civil War, the black jeremiad reflected the strong commitment of African and Anglo Americans to evangelical Protestantism that encouraged blacks to believe that Northern whites would denounce the sin of slavery based upon the promise of a Christian America. Based upon this confidence, a reformist and assimilationist form of protest rhetoric developed by blacks, whites, abolitionists, and progressive reformers called America to live up to its professed ideals in the Constitution, the Declaration of Independence, and the Bible. Utilizing the jeremiad, reformist and assimilationist protest oratory argued against structural flaws in the values of the nation but highlighted the source of slavery and oppression as unfulfilled

11

values of the nation as a demonstration of black loyalty. Moses writes, "The black jeremiad was not simply to provide a verbal outlet for hostilities; it was a means of demonstrating loyalty—both to the principles of egalitarian liberalism and to the Anglo-Christian code of values."[20] The black jeremiad fundamentally operated to affirm the assumptions of American civil religion and, based upon that affirmation, to remind America that it was not living up to its professed ideals, and that, in most cases, blacks were loyal Americans as well. Some blacks believed that they would be included in the American nation based upon their demonstrations of loyalty to the nation and affirmation of American ideals.

One of the components of the black jeremiad was the tradition of black nationalism. Black nationalism arose "simultaneously with the rise of European and American nationalism, from which it borrowed many of its themes."[21] Black nationalism envisioned black people as a chosen people and made sense of the suffering of blacks in slavery as a divine call to bring freedom and dignity in the world. It was hoped and believed that the new millennium (demise of slavery) would be achieved by peaceful means, though some such as Gabriel Prosser, Nat Turner, Denmark Vesey, and others attempted the violent overthrow of slavery.

Blacks were simultaneously integrated into and excluded from American life: they contributed heavily to American society and yet were "non-people" to the white majority. Blacks responded to this duality in American life by developing an American identity that was shaped around the reformist tradition, consistent with the jeremiad, and an alternative identity that was shaped around a more radical non-jeremiadic, black nationalist and separatist tradition. These black nationalists were not convinced that America would turn from the sin of slavery. For the nationalists in this separatist tradition, America had already proven that as a "chosen nation," it had no covenantal duty to include and deal justly with blacks, therefore, confidence in America as a Christian nation and the American jeremiad was an illusion. These voices operated outside the jeremiadic form, adopted their own special mission and destiny for the black race, and utilized this cultural and religious myth as an alternative reality for the empowerment of black

12

people and for inducing social change. For example, Martin Delany, Henry Highland Garnett, Henry McNeal Turner, and Edward Wilmot Blyden in the mid- to late eighteenth and early nineteenth century; Marcus Garvey, Elijah Muhammad, Malcolm X, and Stokely Carmichael (Kwame Toure) in the twentieth century; and Louis Farrakhan in the present, all held a messianic destiny for African Americans running parallel to, and often in conflict with, the messianic destiny of Anglo America. Because there was no promising future in integration and assimilation for blacks in America, the only way to survive was for African Americans to separate, emigrate, or build a base of their own economic independence and enterprise.

The black jeremiad has remained a prime form of discourse addressing the needs and concerns of African Americans from slavery to Jim Crow to the present. The black jeremiad, in its religious or secular form, can be found in the rhetoric of Ida B. Wells, Booker T. Washington, W. E. B. DuBois, Mary McLeod Bethune, Martin Luther King, Jr., Jesse Louis Jackson, Al Sharpton, Alan Keyes, and Barack Obama, to name only a few.[22] From the very beginnings of the African American jeremiad to the present moment, some of the warnings to America were militant and direct, and others were conciliatory, but overwhelmingly blacks used the jeremiad to decry racism and the sin of slavery over and against American ideals.

The roots of the American Dream lie in the concept of the American jeremiad, and the roots of the American jeremiad lie in the European jeremiad and the Old Testament prophets. The American jeremiad shaped the cultural identity of America and established the essential characteristic of the American character as unassailable optimism. The American jeremiad established a tradition of dissent that primarily argued that any issues of economic inequality or racial disparity were a matter of unfulfilled values and not a structural flaw in the American system. As we chart our way out of the Great Recession, it is important to look at the American Dream from the perspective of subjugated and exploited members of American society, those denied the benefit of the American Dream.

CHAPTER TWO

THE CULTURAL MYTH OF AMERICA

"America"... came alive to me as the twin dynamics of empire: on one hand,
a process of violence unparalleled (proportionately) by even the Spanish conquistadors
... on the other hand, an unleashing of creative energies—enterprise,
speculation, community building, personal initiative, industry, confidence,
idealism, and hope—unsurpassed by any other modern nation.
—Sacvan Bercovitch

In the last chapter, we identified the cultural myth of America: a city set on a hill, blessed by God to be the light of the world, with the spiritual values of optimism, hard work, frugality, capitalistic economic striving, and a virgin land as assets to bring the kingdom of God to earth. This cultural myth formed a "centrality" that bound the American nation together in common habits, language, beliefs, and values. Even as cultural myth binds a people together, it also limits their perspective and in some sense blinds them. The blindness in regard to cultural myth is found by asking who in the society is excluded, marginalized, subjugated, domesticated, and, in some cases, even defined as less than human. How does the cultural myth of America function in regard to the respect and treatment of indigenous cultures and people, including groups denied freedom, equality, citizenship, economic participation, voting rights, and so on, in other words, the domination of subjected people?

Some readers may ask why it is necessary to consider the perspective of subjugated and dominated people in this discussion of the American

15

Dream. Consider three important responses. First, unless we want history to be exclusively ideology and propaganda, then historical accuracy is important. Realizing, as Winston Churchill said, that "history is written by the victors," truth is important to the progress and forward movement of any particular people and human history, lest we are doomed to repeat the mistakes of the past. If our history is to be anything more than dogma and indoctrination, subjugation and domination as a factual part of the American Dream must be discussed.

Second, protest movements of subjugated people compel a society either to live up to its stated values, reformulate said values, or ferment revolution and overthrow. For example, consider the American value of freedom. Subjugated people keep freedom free. Langston Hughes, in a poem entitled "Democracy," writes, "Freedom is a strong seed planted in a great need."[1] Many human beings, once possessing a measure of freedom, tend to protect their privilege and conserve the benefit to themselves. As a result, the human tendency is to either intentionally or by sheer blindness exclude others. It takes the protest of those who have been denied freedom ("a strong seed planted in a great need") to pressure the cultural, political, and economic boundaries in the way that is necessary for America to live up to its expressed ideal of freedom.

Third, given that the purpose of this book is to cause an uprising of ordinary American citizens, particularly pastors, congregations, and all people of goodwill to reclaim the American Dream, I am openly and unapologetically engaging in dissent. The cultural myth of America fosters and allows dissent, but even in allowing it, there is dissent that the nation considers appropriate and dissent that is perceived as a threat. On the whole, dissent has moved the cultural myth forward to greater levels of inclusion and freedom for subjugated groups and dissent has been co-opted to perpetuate and entrench the very cultural myth dissent is fighting against. I am mindful that even as I call for an uprising of ordinary American citizens to reclaim the American Dream from its economic stronghold, there is the possibility of co-optation and further entrenchment of the very economic stranglehold I am protesting against. In other words, the plasticity of the cultural myth of America is its ability to co-opt dissent into middle-class culture to protect against structural and fundamental change and protect the status quo. I want to guard against this distinct possibility by identification of its existence from the very start of this discussion. With this as background, I want to look at the cultural myth of America in regard to indigenous and subjugated people.

The Cultural Myth of America and Imperialism

Based in America's cultural myth and identity, I define America's attitude and treatment of the land and the indigenous people of America as "imperialism." Comparing the Canadian and American myth of cultural identity, Bercovitch suggests:

> "Canada" was the *colonial* version of the myth, a story told by invaders who claimed authority for conquest from abroad— from European royalty, a civilization centered in England and France. "America" was the indigenous *imperialist* inversion. It relocated the seat of empire from the Old World to the New; it reversed the very meaning of "newness" from its colonial status of dependency to a declaration not just of independence, but of superiority (political, moral, even spiritual); and in this new sense sanctified the "empty continent" as itself constituting the natural-divine patent for conquest.[2]

The cultural myth of America ritualized imperialism as a critical element of American identity. While imperialism is part of the cultural myth of America, it is not the entirety of American identity and character. Following Bercovitch, I subscribe to a more balanced perspective on American character and identity:

> As I followed its [the American cultural myth's] changing terms of identity (Puritan errand, national mission, Manifest Destiny, the dream) the windings of language turned out to be matters of history. "America" as an act of symbolic appropriation came alive to me as the twin dynamics of empire: on one hand, a process of violence unparalleled (proportionately) by even the Spanish conquistadors and sustained in the twentieth century by a rhetoric of holy war against everything un-American; on the other hand, an unleashing of creative energies—enterprise, speculation, community building, personal initiative, industry, confidence,

17

idealism, and hope—unsurpassed by any other modern nation. What I discovered in the interconnections between violence and culture formation was transcendence in action: "America," an interpretation, through which the worlds out there had been triumphantly repressed, rhetorically and historically—first, by the myths of their inhabitants ("savage," "primitive") attended by the facts of genocide and then by symbols of the land ("virgin," "wilderness") attended by the creation of the United States as "America."[3]

A balanced perspective on America suggests that America has released more creative energy into the world than any modern nation and yet has also been imperialistic and violent on an unparalleled level. The cultural myth of America celebrates the "industry, confidence, idealism, hope" of America and often ignores the effects of imperialism, such as violence, racism, slavery, genocide, and the conquest of indigenous people. The cultural myth of America creates an "ideological consensus" involving American exceptionalism and "an increasingly pervasive middle-class hegemony" that has a difficult time facing the dynamics of imperialism such as genocide, violence, racism, and slavery.[4] Dissent expressed through the American jeremiad is an American tradition that fosters and is a part of middle-class hegemony, while dissent that operates outside of the American jeremiad finds a much more difficult hearing in America and is co-opted by the plasticity of the cultural myth of America to protect middle-class culture from structural and fundamental change. The perspectives of indigenous people and subjugated people represent a tradition of dissent to the cultural myth of America.

The American Tradition of Dissent

Despite the ideological middle-class consensus, American dissent is tolerated and encouraged, as long as the dissent falls within the constraints of the American jeremiad and calls, as Kaveny says, "the New Jerusalem to repent, so that it can continue its progress to eternal and temporal flourishing."[5] The ritual form of the American jeremiad ensures that a *certain kind* of dissent can be absorbed into middle-class culture and the maintenance of American values:

The plight of the mid-nineteenth-century feminists is instructive. On the one hand, it reminds us *that the jeremiad has always restricted the ritual of consensus to a certain group within the culture.* When William Arthur spoke of "the American," he was not thinking of people like Margaret Fuller—or for that matter, of Frederick Douglass, Black Hawk, Rabbi Issac Meyer Wise, of John England, the Catholic Bishop of South Carolina . . . the fact is that the American consensus could also absorb feminism, so long as that would lead into the middle-class American Way. Blacks and Indians too could learn to be True Americans, when in the fullness of time, they would adopt the tenets of black and red capitalism. John Brown could join Adams, Franklin, and Jefferson in the pantheon of Revolutionary heroes when it was understood that he wanted to fulfill rather than undermine the American dream.[6]

Bercovitch offers the critical insight that *the jeremiad has always restricted the ritual of consensus to a certain group within the culture.* In other words, the jeremiad has limited the ritual of consensus to those of middle-class values and culture and excluded Native Americans, free Blacks, slaves, Jews, immigrants, women, and so on. Michael Novak argues that the "adolescent American dream is ethnocentric," that is, "its primary symbols are white Anglo American, Protestant, and male." In accordance with American exceptionalism, Novak concludes that "the central axis of world history, according to this [American] dream, pivots on the history of the Anglo-American race."[7] Some in the contemporary audience suggest that different groups that are not white Anglo American, Protestant, and male have been included in the American Dream, particularly evidenced by the presidential candidacy of Hillary Clinton and the presidency of Barack Obama, such that Novak's comments are no longer relevant. Notice Novak's use of the word *adolescent,* meaning that the American Dream can mature to include, based upon protest and dissent across time, some of the very people who were once excluded. Whether or not we have matured is a subject of debate not within the scope of this book. What is most essential is to recognize the access point to the American Dream is the adoption of the "middle-class American way," which is the tenet of capitalism. Even John Brown, a radical and revolutionary abolitionist, who practiced armed insurrection in the 1850s to abolish slavery, could become an American if he adopted capitalism and wanted to fulfill rather than undermine the American Dream. This is quite an incredible statement: John Brown, who some would label a "terrorist," if he would only adopt capitalism, can join John Adams, Benjamin Franklin, and Thomas Jefferson in the distinguished pantheon of American revolutionary heroes. One becomes a "true American" by adopting the middle-class way of American capitalism, and thereby clearly demonstrating that one desires to fulfill rather than undermine the American Dream. By implication, if one does not adopt the middle-class way of American capitalism, then one is not an "American."

The American jeremiad, the cultural myth of America, and the middle-class American way are inherently conservative and function to preserve the status quo, which is the ritual of benefit for a certain group within the culture.[8] The acceptable form of American dissent reinforces the cultural myth of America by making clear that any challenge to American values is not based on structural flaws or defects in American values; it is rather a matter of human fault in the nonfulfillment of the stated values. John M. Murphy argues that "the jeremiad limits the scope of reform and the depth of social criticism."[9] Instead of questioning American values, jeremiadic speakers call the public back to American values as a way to bring "good out of evil" and assure the covenant of America. As an example, Murphy critiques Robert F. Kennedy:

> Even though many Americans saw Robert Kennedy as a radical, he stood squarely within the American jeremiadic tradition. While he certainly spoke to and for radicals and outcasts in American society, he proposed that they enter American society on his terms. They would move up and out of poverty as Kennedy's family had done: by embracing the premises and values of the American Dream. The system itself did not need radical change.[10]

Instead of calling into question American values, the American jeremiad calls the public back to traditional American values (middle-class American way and capitalism) and assures the promise of America. Murphy suggests that, given America's checkered racial history, it is especially difficult to achieve social change by relying on precepts of the past and traditional values when the issue is American racism.[11] Murphy makes the argument that, especially in regard to race, the American jeremiad may "limit the political choices of the audience."[12] Later, I demonstrate that in the last years of his life Martin Luther King, Jr., articulated structural flaws in the American system. The conservative form of the American jeremiad restricted the depth of King's social critique; therefore, King abandoned the American jeremiad and sought to radically reorient the cultural myth of America.

What happens when dissent moves beyond the argument of unfulfilled values and finds fault in the structural values of America, the very cultural myth of America itself? Can the conservatism of the jeremiad and the cultural myth of America sustain radical social critique? What if the critique is that the poor and the middle class do not have access to the American Dream? What if the factual reality that only the smallest percent at the top have had access to the American Dream in the last thirty years is not a matter of unfulfilled values, but a fault at the structural level with American values? The pattern is that any criticism of this nature that challenges the structural values of America must be co-opted. Let's look at the co-optation of dissent outside of the American jeremiad.

The Co-optation of Dissent

As stated, the plasticity of the cultural myth of America is its ability to co-opt dissent into middle-class culture to protect against structural and fundamental change and safeguard the status quo. The middle-class way of American capitalism has the ability to absorb dissent that is outside of the American jeremiad and co-opt it to serve the purposes of preservation of the cultural myth of America. But the current reality of the Great Recession in America demands a critique outside the American jeremiad and at the level of the structural values of America. The process of co-optation of dissent guards against this uprising of ordinary American citizens to reclaim the American Dream from its economic stronghold and attempts to absorb this dissent into the middle-class American way.

In the same way that we developed a balanced critique of America as creative and imperialistic, it is necessary to find balance in dissent outside the jeremiad and move away from the traditional dichotomy, when talking about dissent, of selling out versus outright rejection of the system. The issue is not the essentialist perspective of co-optation (selling out to the system) versus dissent (rejection of the system), but the ability of the cultural myth of America to engage in varieties of cooptation and dissent, or a blurring of the lines that define co-optation and dissent. How can one be fundamentally against a culture (whatever that means) and ignore the fact that one is fundamentally a part of the culture that one is against? What does dissent mean when dissent is against the very cultural myth that gives one the right to dissent? What does dissent mean when one uses the rhetoric and values of the dominant culture that one is dissenting against? The cultural myth of America muddies the waters of dissent between radicalism and reform into varieties of co-optation and dissent because the right of dissent and the materials, symbols, and language of dissent come from the cultural myth of America. The one who dissents is in a conundrum. So let's look at the process of co-optation.

The first step in the process of the cultural myth of America's co-optation of dissent is the creation of dissent. To its credit, the cultural myth of America allows and fosters dissent by values such as freedom of speech, freedom of the press, and so on. In fact such libertarian dissent is essential to the cultural myth of America based upon the fact that America was founded on dissent related to the power structures of Europe. It is in the DNA of America to dissent ("Don't tread on me!"). The assimilation of formerly excluded groups such as homosexuals is at least in part due to the ability of advocates to frame the argument on libertarian grounds.

Many cultures meet dissent with violent resistance and extreme measures of intimidation such as murder, imprisonment, rape, torture, and so on. America meets dissent outside the American jeremiad with violence as well, but there is a much subtler process of co-optation that operates. America generates "alternative Americas," radical alternatives to America that challenge the structural values of America such as those generated by Nat Turner, Paul Robeson, Elizabeth Cady Stanton,

Angela Davis, Malcolm X, John Brown, Angelina and Sarah Grimke, and Martin Luther King, Jr., to name a few.

The second step is to co-opt the alternative Americas to reaffirm original American ideals and therefore harness revolution for American purposes.[13] "America" generates and even induces dissent but then co-opts the dissent into conservative patterns of culture. Co-optation becomes possible because in order to oppose the system, one must use the ideals of the system. Dissent is forced to use the rhetoric and values of the cultural myth of America and, in using the rhetoric and values, reinforce the very myth that advocates of social change resist. Dissenters end up opposing the system in ways that reaffirm its ideals:

> hence, the ambiguities that linked Douglass to King, Stanton to Steinem, Thoreau to Goodman. In all these cases, dissent was demonstrably an appeal to, and through, the rhetoric and values of the dominant culture and it issued in a fundamental challenge to the system; racism subverted in the story of a self-made man; patriarchy subverted through a revised version of the Declaration of Independence; the authority of government subverted by a Fourth of July experiment in self-reliance.[14]

Given America's checkered racial history, it is especially difficult to achieve social change by relying on precepts of the past and traditional American values when the issue is American racism because racism is often subverted and co-opted into the myth of the self-made man. An example of this subversion is the exchange between Chairman Francis E. Walter and Paul Robeson during Robeson's appearance before the House Un-American Activities Committee, June 12, 1956:[15]

> THE CHAIRMAN: Now, what prejudice are you talking about? You were graduated from Rutgers and you were graduated from the University of Pennsylvania. . . . There was no prejudice against you. Why did you not send your son to Rutgers?

> Mr. ROBESON: Just a moment. This is something that I challenge very deeply, and very sincerely: that the success of a few Negroes, including myself or Jackie Robinson can make up . . . for seven hundred dollars a year for thousands of Negro families in the South. My father was a slave, and I have cousins who are

23

sharecroppers, and I do not see my success in terms of myself. That is the reason my own success has not meant what it should mean: I have sacrificed literally hundreds of thousands, if not millions, of dollars for what I believe in.[16]

The subtle implication of the chairman's question was that Robeson's success proved that each individual person could be successful regardless of race and that there was no such phenomenon as racism. Oppression is personal suffering and success is individual accomplishment, and therefore the American Dream is possible for blacks, if only they would work hard enough to achieve it. Robeson refused to allow the Horatio Alger myth of the self-made man to co-opt and disregard the mistreatment of millions of American blacks based upon the success of one token black person. His statement, "I do not see success in terms of myself," is an indication of a different values proposition than the American myth of the self-made man.

Martin Luther King, Jr., in the 1967 speech "Beyond Vietnam," as we will discuss later, moves outside the jeremiad and challenges the values of American exceptionalism. American exceptionalism, the imperialistic belief in the vision of "a city set up on a hill," is a rhetorical strategy of cohesion, the "centrality" that holds the society together. King critiqued the very values and identity of America and received virtually universal American contempt and condemnation. King's radical call for a "revolution of values" is co-opted by the singular deification of King in American popular culture standing on the steps of the Lincoln monument in 1963 reciting "I have a dream" because it reinforces the cultural myth of America. King is admitted to the pantheon of American heroes' memorials on the National Mall, along with the Washington Monument, the Lincoln Memorial, the Thomas Jefferson Memorial, the World War II Memorial, the Franklin Delano Roosevelt Memorial, the Korean War Veterans Memorial, and the Vietnam Veterans Memorial, because of his endorsement of the cultural myth of America in 1963. Popular culture gives no evidence of King's anti-Vietnam stance and call for revolution based upon a structural critique of the values of America. Even as cultural myth binds a people together, it also limits their perspective and in some sense blinds them. The blindness in regard to cultural myth is found by asking who in the society is excluded, marginalized, subjugated, domesticated, and, in some cases, even defined as less than human. The critique of subjugated groups, as long as it operates within the American jeremiad, moves America to include groups heretofore excluded and to allow, as Kaveny says, "the New Jerusalem to repent, so that it can continue its progress to eternal and temporal flourishing." But there are times when the values of the nation must be critiqued outside of the American jeremiad. The Great Recession is such an occasion. What is required is a reconceptualization of the identity and values of the nation. Understanding the possibility of co-optation, let's now evaluate the fall of the American Dream.

CHAPTER THREE

THE FALL OF THE AMERICAN DREAM

Now look, you built a factory and it turned into something terrific, or a great idea—
God bless. Keep a big hunk of it. But part of the underlying social contract is you take a
hunk of that and pay forward for the next kid who comes along.
—Elizabeth Warren

Statistics are clear that for the last thirty years only the top 1 percent of Americans have had access to the American Dream.[1] The overwhelming majority of the rest of Americans have suffered unemployment, wage stagnation, standard of living decline, and an increase in the levels of poverty. The result of values, policies, and practices of the last thirty years is the decline of the American Dream for the average American citizen.

One major set of factors in the decline is that we now live in a less U.S.-centric, more knowledge-driven, and more competitive world. India and China are rising as financial powers, and it is projected that by the year 2020, if not sooner, China will be the world's largest economy. Several nations are now outpacing America in education, science, engineering, and skill development, not to mention the availability of a cheaper labor pool with fewer benefits and responsibilities, which is attractive to global capital. Technology and the Internet have made knowledge digital and portable and not confined to any nation or locale. The world is a more competitive place, and the American worker and American business are contending in a global environment that America has never known before.

It is easy solely to focus on the global environment and discuss the decline of the American Dream from economic, social, political, and educational perspectives. Others, much more qualified in these areas, are already giving critical analysis and making perceptive recommendations. Besides the influence of the external environment, there is a second, internal set of factors in the decline of the American Dream: the status, nature, and condition of American values.

The exaggerated view of capitalistic economic striving as part of the cultural myth of America has come fundamentally to define the person as a consumer. This value, this consumerist definition of human personality, has led to the demise of the American Dream for the overwhelming majority of American citizens. Remember, the purpose of this book is to cause an uprising of ordinary American citizens, particularly pastors, their congregations, and people of goodwill to reclaim the American Dream from its exclusively economic stranglehold on the nation. The role of the church is to define human personality from a biblical, and therefore healthier and more healing, perspective. The church can offer unique insightful expertise in the question of values. The church must ask questions about the nature and ultimate endgame of American national values.

Americans are defined and define themselves as consumers. My daughter, as a young college student, was dating a football player. She invited me to line up with her at 5:00 A.M. on a Saturday morning at a popular shoe factory store to purchase a pair of shoes for her boyfriend as a birthday present. She told me that the store did not open until 10:00 A.M., but she needed to get there at 5:00 A.M. to make sure she got the right size shoe. Of course, I refused because this level of brand consciousness as a value offended my sensibilities. I woke up the next morning at 5:00 A.M., and she was gone. Suddenly, I had visions of her out there by herself and in serious danger. If she were harmed, I would be complicit in her mother's eyes because I had refused to go. I immediately called her, and she told me that she was in no danger and that there were "people as far as the eye could see," as well as three policemen to keep order. After waiting for five hours and finally entering the store, she returned with the shoes, and only because her boyfriend wore a larger size. Standard sizes were sold out. She described the sea of humanity that was in line for the shoes. I asked her if she would take me to see the sight, given the fact that this offering of discount shoes occurs every two weeks.

Two weeks later, I got out there and saw more people than I could have imagined lined up at 5:00 A.M. There were indeed three policemen to keep order. I lamented the difficulty that I had with what I was seeing. I said to her that I was going to show her the price of this shoe outfitter's stock when I got back home. I showed her that the price of the stock was $50.00 per share. The shoes were more expensive than the stock, and, I would guess, not one of these young people had experience in stock ownership. I told my daughter that these young people had been trained to be consumers; they had been trained to consume so that others could build capital while they remained broke.

With such consumerist values and training in our culture, it was normal and explainable to me that a few had so much while so many had so little. I speculated that no one had explained to these young people that the stock was cheaper and more valuable than the shoes. I wondered if they had been exposed to the reality of depreciating and appreciating assets and the fact that one will never build wealth with depreciating assets.

Of course, consumerism is not predicated upon age or race. I went to an outlet mall and saw women of all races and ages in line at a designer purse outlet store. I wondered how many women in line owned any stock in the company that they were buying the purses from. In other words, how much capital did these purchases accrue for these women? I write this on the eve of the consumer post-Thanksgiving "Black Friday" marketing season. When I see people lining up at midnight to buy things, I ask the same question: how many of these people buying televisions, toys, clothes, games, and so on have any stock ownership? I have children and I have stood in lines to get goods so that they could have a wonderful Christmas, so I am not casting apersions on anyone. I am analyzing the values and how and why it is that so many of the have-nots have less and the haves have more. It is a difficult question, and it must be asked of all of us: how many of these purchases build capital and wealth for the people making the purchase? Based upon the cultural myth of America, the majority of American people have been defined as consumers and have been trained to build wealth for the producers at their own expense. Let's look critically at how the average American comes to be defined as a consumer.

Americans As Consumers

In 1931, James Trunslow Adams, Pulitzer Prize–winning writer and historian, wrote *Epic of America*, a one-volume popular history of America that offers a well-defined treatise on the foundations of the American nation and an insightful analysis of American character. Adams coins the phrase "American Dream," critiques American materialism, and laments that the essentials of American character, thrift, and hard work are fading away. Because I believe his critique of the American Dream is true, insightful, and still very relevant today, I want to look closely at his thinking.

As stated, Adams initially defined the American Dream as "a better, richer, and happier life for all our citizens of every rank." In the American environment, the words *richer and happier life* could be construed as support for the consumerist definition of human personality, where "richer" is equated with a happier life and commonly known as "making it big" or "striking it rich." Later in his book, he clarifies his definition:

> But there has been also the *American dream*, that dream of a land in which life should be better and richer and fuller for every man, with opportunity for each according to his ability or achievement. . . . It is not a dream of motor cars and high wages merely, but a dream of a social order in which each man and each woman shall be able to attain to the fullest stature of which they are innately capable, and be recognized by others for what they are regardless of the fortuitous circumstances of birth or position.[2]

Adams clarifies that the American Dream is not a dream merely of material plenty, though he admits that this counted heavily in the attraction of tens of millions to America. The dream of America is the ability to grow to one's full stature as a human being without repression by social orders or structures of class. Adams expresses the opportunity and idealism of the American Dream, a dream, according to Adams, that is not duplicated anywhere in the world.

Although recognizing the opportunity and idealism of the American Dream, Adams does not overlook the ugly scars left on Americans by three centuries of exploitation and conquest of the North American continent, or what he calls "our scramble for the untold wealth which lay at the foot of the rainbow":

> We came to insist upon business and money-making and material improvement as good in themselves; how they took on aspects of moral virtues; how we came to think an unthinking optimism essential; how we refused to look on the seamy and sordid realities of any situation in which we found ourselves; . . . how size and statistics of material development came to be more important in our eyes than quality and spiritual values.[3]

Adams recognizes the endgame of American values when he postulates that American focus on the size and statistics of material development led to the exploitation and conquest of the continent and the diminishment of quality and spiritual values in American life.

Adams argues that by the 1930s, Americans no longer had the frontier to divert attention and absorb energy. By then, Americans had moved beyond acquiring a bare living and setting up a fair economic base, and the American Dream opened up to the question of values. Besides this progress, while Americans were absorbed in the task of exploitation and conquest, the world changed.

As contemporary twenty-first-century Americans face the critical change of a less U.S.-centric world, what Adams said then is true today: when dealing with change, values are of prime importance. Faced with tremendous global change, the question of American life in the 1930s was the question of values. Adams makes this point by asking: "It is easy to say, a better and richer life for all, but what is better and what is richer?"[4] The response to the question of what is better and what is richer is a discussion of values.

Adams addresses the question of values when he asks, for what purpose do Americans want to make higher wages and become richer? Is it to create a better person by increasing leisure and the opportunity to make use of it, or is it for the sole purpose of increasing one's power as a "consumer"? His argument in the 1930s is reminiscent of what we hear today: Americans are warned that if they do not consume themselves to the limit, and "stimulate the economy," they might not have jobs and high wages at all. "Instead of indulging in pleasures that do not cost money," Adams comments, the American appears "to be getting into a treadmill in which he earns, not that he may enjoy, but that he may speak, in order that the owners of the factories may grow richer."[5] When human values are defined as producer and consumer, then the more ruthlessly efficient big business is, supposedly the better it is for everybody. For Adams, many consumer goods do make us better, but the definition of the human being as consumer is destructive. The human being must first be defined as a human being, only incidentally as a consumer, and then we must discern what values are most satisfying when we define ourselves as human beings. Adams believes that we do not create a high-wage earner so that he or she may consume more, "but that he or she may live more abundantly, whether by enjoying those things which are factory-produced or not."[6] The contrasting views of the human being as human being, and human being as consumer, generate values that are entirely different socially and economically.

When we value human beings as consumers, we move away from a nation of strong individuals in which one can hold individual thoughts and opinions to a nation of "employees" who are dependent upon the whims of their employers:

> Steadily, we are tending toward becoming a nation of employees—whether a man gets five dollars a day or a hundred thousand a year. The "yes-men" are as new to our national life as to our vocabulary, but they are real. It is no longer merely the laborer or factory hand who is dependent on the whim of his employer, but men all the way up the economic and social scale.[7]

From Adams's perspective, an almost irresistible economic pressure is brought to bear on the workers to adjust their work to the needs of business and a mass consumption that lowers the quality of thought and expression. All of this is the result of the fact that America has become a nation of "employees."

Another result of Americans becoming a nation of "employees" is a marked injustice in distribution of the total income of individuals.

Wealth is a social product and should be equitably controlled and distributed in the interests of society. Adams is not against wealth; rather, he asserts that values direct wealth. When wealth is directed by the values of consumerism, it does one thing, and when directed by a different set of values, it does something else. He argues that until we settle on the values of life, with the discussion of wealth, "we are likely to attack in a wrong direction and burn the barn to find the penny in our hay."[8] There is a positive value to wealth when wealth is directed by the appropriate national values.

Elizabeth Warren, candidate in the 2012 United States Senate election in Massachusetts, took a similar position on the purpose of wealth in America. Warren believes that nobody gets rich on their own. The American public pays for the education of workers that the factory owner hires to help them make their wealth, for the roads that move the goods to market, and for the safety and security provided by the police and fire forces. Warren says:

> You built a factory out there? Good for you. But I want to be clear: you moved your goods to market on the roads the rest of us paid for; you hired workers the rest of us paid to educate. . . . Now look, you built a factory and it turned into something terrific, or a great idea—God bless. Keep a big hunk of it. But part of the underlying social contract is you take a hunk of that and pay forward for the next kid who comes along.[9]

Both Adams and Warren believe that wealth is a social product. The philanthropy that operates in American culture is to "merely return, not unwisely, a part of their wealth to that society without which they could not have made it, and which too often they have plundered in the making."[10] Adams does not blame individuals; he believes that it has to do with the values of the system as a whole:

> A system that steadily increases the gulf between the ordinary man and the super-rich, that permits the resources of society to be gathered into personal fortunes that afford their owners millions of income a year, with only the chance that here and there a few may be moved to confer some of their surplus upon the public in ways chosen wholly by themselves, is assuredly a

wasteful and unjust system. It is, perhaps, as inimical as anything could be to the American dream. I do not belittle the generosity or public spirit of certain men. It is the system that as yet is at fault. Nor is it likely to be voluntarily altered by those who benefit most by it. No ruling class has ever willingly abdicated. Democracy can never be saved, and would not be worth saving, unless it can save itself.[11]

The national values that allow an increasing gulf between the ordinary person and the super-rich and the resulting system of the philanthropy of a few, he defines as being "inimical," that is, unfriendly and hostile to the American Dream. He urges an uprising of ordinary American citizens to save the American Dream. An uprising is necessary because those that benefit the most by this value system will never voluntarily alter it. Echoing the words of Frederick Douglass that "power concedes nothing without a demand,"[12] Adams concludes that democracy, if it is worth saving, must save itself. Ordinary Americans must rise up, redefine national values and themselves as other than consumers, and save democracy from the excesses of capitalism.

Without a new clarity on national values, citizens are left to trust in "the wise paternalism of politicians and the infinite wisdom of business leaders."[13] Without the development of "greatness" in the individual souls of citizens, citizens will look to the government or the heads of the great corporations to define a satisfying and humane existence. Adams states:

> Until countless men and woman have decided in their own hearts, through experience and perhaps disillusion, what is a genuinely satisfying life, a "good life" in the old Greek sense, we need to look to neither political nor business leaders.[14]

Adams's point is that without a change in consumerist values that express contentment with multiplying our material possessions and "keeping up with the Joneses," then we can never expect our politicians or business leaders "to become spiritual leaders of a democracy that despises spiritual things."[15] So long as wealth and power are our sole badges of success, it is useless generally to expect a politician or business leader to rise above the source of his or her power. Adams argues that "Americans must understand that just because a person is born with a particular knack for gathering in vast aggregates of money and power for himself, he may not on that account be the wisest leader to follow nor the best fitted to propound a sane philosophy of life."[16]

While politicians and business leaders have a seat at the table of the discussion of values, the church must play a vital, critical, and even leading role. The Christian church has a tremendous amount to say regarding the question of values, the "development of greatness in the souls of people," or defining what is a "good life." And although some parts of the Christian church have endorsed the consumerist paradigm of human personality, what is truly needed is for the American church to define a humane and satisfying existence outside of the producer/consumer paradigm that presently dominates American life. It is the redefinition of these values that is the aim of this work. Citizens cannot curb, guide, or control great business interests and the powers of government without a clear purpose based upon a humane set of values. Hence, we need the church in its prophetic role to establish true and humane values. I want to now look at the prophetic politics of the church and the American Dream.

SECTION TWO

PROPHETIC POLITICS AND THE AMERICAN DREAM

In the early part of the twenty-first century, when the American Dream has collapsed for all but a few, I call for dissent, an uprising of excluded ordinary Americans to oppose the stranglehold of the economic interpretation of the American Dream on the nation. Because the argument against the economic interpretation of the American Dream is ultimately a question of values—specifically, whether the human being is valued as a human being or singularly as a producer/consumer—the church has a vital, unique, and leading role to play in the dissent. It is the role of the church to define what a satisfying and humane existence is and to raise its voice in dissent when those definitions are not evident in the church and culture. Those who raise their voices on behalf of the church, and sometimes even to the church, are called prophets. I look at two prophets of the church—Martin Luther King, Jr., and Jeremiah A. Wright, Jr.—because those who would operate as prophets would do well to learn valuable lessons from their dissent. Chapter 4, entitled "Prophetic Reformation: Martin Luther King, Jr., and the Triumphant March to the American Dream," examines King's support and endorsement of the American Dream. Chapter 5 discusses King's radical critique of American values in his 1967 speech "Beyond Vietnam." Chapter 6 considers the media's co-optation of the message of radical prophets and is entitled "Prophetic Transformation: Jeremiah A. Wright, Jr., and the American Dream." Although Barack Obama is not a prophet like King and Wright, I also look at his speech "A More Perfect Union," his vision of a prophetic resolution to the twin dynamics of American empire. It is important to begin our discussion with helping the reader understand the concepts of prophetic politics and the radical reformist jeremiad.

Prophetic Politics

Paul D. Hanson develops what he calls a Christian political theology and names it "prophetic politics."[1] Hanson lists five political models represented in the Old Testament, the most significant of which is the prophetic political model:

> The prophetic political model embodies the primacy of faith over human agency and temporal institutions. . . . The prophets

entered every political dialogue by stating clearly the necessary grounding of every political strategy in submission to God's universal suzerainty. Complete trust in God was the quality without which prophetic politics was impossible. The inevitable concomitant of the ascription of absolute rule to God alone was the relativization of every human institution.[2]

Hanson then lists the cardinal characteristics of the prophetic model. He does not list them in the manner stated below, but in the attempt to quickly synthesize his thought, I have summarized:

1. Unqualified Allegiance to God's Domain—While refusing to endorse any political ideology as identical with God's eternal rule, prophetic politics demands of all people of faith, regardless of their host governments, unqualified allegiance to God's universal domain. It is from this perspective of allegiance to God's universal domain that the prophets critique the present order.

2. The Divine Call to Advocate for God's Reign—Prophetic politics is for those who have received the divine call to advocate for the standards of God's universal divine reign that transcends all human boundaries. It is impossible to understand a prophet or prophecy until one grasps the prophet's sense of divine reign and a call to represent that reign on earth.

3. Human Governance Outside of God's Reign—The prophet's task is to remind a nation that its structures of governance are not identical with divine rule. If a government is to survive, it must articulate both domestic and foreign policy consistent with moral principles in line with the will of God that transcend partisan politics and nationalistic self-interest.

4. Prophets Are Not Popular—On behalf of the universal and sovereign God, prophets speak with a consistency that rattles earthly kings, high priests, and governments. Because their silence cannot be purchased, they expect rebuke, vilification, violence, and even death.

In summation, those who ascribe to prophetic politics "give expression to their patriotism by ascribing to their government limited, penultimate authority, while reserving their ultimate allegiance for the universal sovereign, the Creator God of all nations."[3]

Although prophetic politics may sometimes utilize the American jeremiad, such as in King's "I Have a Dream" speech, there are other instances in which prophetic politics moves outside the American jeremiad. The American jeremiad features an unshakeable optimism and inverts vengeance and judgment into a promise of national success. Some in the tradition of prophetic politics, more in line with the European jeremiad, reject unshakeable optimism and announce judgment and destruction without the inherent promise of national vindication. I want to look more closely at prophetic politics that embraces the American jeremiad and prophetic politics that moves outside the American jeremiad. I start with Martin Luther King, Jr., who, in the first years of his ministry, adopted the cultural myth of America and adopted a radical reformist jeremiad.

Radical Reformist Jeremiad

For many, from the years 1954 to 1965, King was the most persuasive voice that stirred the conscience of the American nation to live up to its ideals. To many, King was an American hero. Certainly not all Americans regarded King this way, especially in the South, but King received much positive press, culminating in the immense notoriety of the "Letter from Birmingham City Jail," the "I Have a Dream" speech, and his winning of the Nobel Peace Prize in 1964. During this period, King became a national and international hero. He endorsed the cultural myth of America and therefore was in basic agreement with the values of the majority of the American public.

In his early discourse, from 1954 to 1965, Martin Luther King, Jr., utilized a radical reformist jeremiad. It was radical because it challenged and induced fundamental social change within the American system. It was reformist because King's social change, consistent with the American jeremiad, fully sanctioned and celebrated the American Dream. The radical reformist jeremiad endorsed the cultural myth of

America because it postulated that difficulties in America are based in America not living up to its professed values and ideals, and not based in structural flaws in the system. The American public and King agreed on four pivotal assumptions: (1) the American system is basically good, as evidenced by the values of freedom, justice, and morality; (2) the American Dream is the most effective symbology for placing blacks in American society and for illustrating that whites and blacks are in the same universe of values; (3) faults in America, such as racism and segregation, are not indicative of systemic failure but are rooted in unfulfilled values; and (4) acceptable protest is to participate in the American jeremiad, that is, the mainstream of American dissent (for example, the abolitionists and progressive reformers), whose ideas and strategies for social change were a celebration of the values of the culture and of change within the status quo. I want to look at the radical reformist jeremiad of Martin Luther King, Jr., through a close reading of his March 25, 1965, Montgomery, Alabama, speech, "Our God Is Marching On."

CHAPTER FOUR

PROPHETIC REFORMATION: MARTIN LUTHER KING, JR., AND THE TRIUMPHANT MARCH TO THE AMERICAN DREAM

With nineteen jeeps, four military trucks in rear escort, and two helicopters hovering above, on March 21, 1965, at 12:46 p.m., an estimated three thousand marchers, including Martin Luther King, Jr., left Selma on their way to Montgomery, Alabama. Although actual marcher numbers are disputed, numbers swelled as they walked the last four miles into Montgomery. They passed St. Jude Catholic Hospital, where Coretta Scott King had given birth to the first two King children, and Holt Street Baptist Church, where at age twenty-six King had given his famous address to the first mass meeting of the bus boycott.[1] They passed Court Square, where Rosa Parks boarded the bus on which she was arrested, which started the boycott. They converged at Dexter Avenue Baptist Church, the site of King's first pastorate. With the state capitol now in view, they staged a rally from a flatbed truck. Andrew Young and Ralph Abernathy led the mass meeting; songs were sung and testimonials were given. Rosa Parks and others addressed the mass meeting. And then King rose to speak. Like the March on

Washington, but never again in his lifetime, networks transmitted the full speech nationwide. He told the assembled crowd and nation, "Our God Is Marching On."[2]

"Our God Is Marching On"

It is not surprising, given the experience of marching from Selma to Montgomery, that the image of walking dominates the speech. The speech has thirty-six paragraphs, counting the entire closing "How long? Not long!" peroration as one paragraph. Of the thirty-six paragraphs, the metaphor of walking or some derivative is mentioned in nineteen paragraphs, more than half. Aside from *walk* or *walking,* King uses *feet, stride, move, march, tread, pilgrimage, trampling,* and *ain't gon' let nobody turn us around.* The key movements of the speech can be plotted as the journey from feet to walk to move to march to victory.

In this same vein, King calls the process of the struggle for freedom a triumphant march. He is both describing the process of victory from Selma to Montgomery and encouraging his audience to continue the march to the full rights of American citizenship. The struggle for civil rights is a triumphal march to the American Dream, and victory progresses from feet to walking to moving (striding) to marching to victory.

King starts in paragraph 1 with the walking metaphor. Then, in paragraph 2, he moves to a now-classic story about a seventy-year-old black woman who was walking in the Montgomery bus boycott and was asked if she needed a ride. She responded, "My feets is tired, but my soul is rested."[3] In paragraph 3, speaking of the opposition, King says that "they" told us that "we" wouldn't get here, and those who said we'd make it over only over their dead bodies.[4] King refutes the opposition by declaring victory before the forces of power in Alabama and proclaims that we won't let anybody turn us around.[5] Of course, this is a metaphor of walking and movement, expressing determination to overcome all obstacles, the song and phrase residing deep in the Negro struggle for freedom.

In paragraph 16, King says that now we are on the move, no wave of racism can stop us. Even burning down our churches will not stop us.[6]

In paragraph 17, he proceeds from moving to marching. After he calls for the continuation of the triumphant march to the American Dream, he says that we will now march on segregated housing in every ghetto, and until we can live side by side in decent housing.[7]

King does nine more anaphoric "let us march" phrases from paragraphs 17 to 24, or ten by including one signals marching to the realization of the American dream. When King says "Let us," rhetorically he is beginning his ascendancy to a celebrative and uplifting close. King makes ten anaphoric "let us" phrases and starts the emotional ascension to the climactic close. In paragraph 25, King uses Joshua to illustrate that walking and marching around Jericho brought victory,[8] and King equates marching with victory and the fact that the "battle am" in the hands of marchers. King then builds on the "battle am in my hand" in paragraph 28.[9] In other words, some suggest that King and colleagues (Joshua) should not "fit the battle of Jericho" and that King and colleagues (Joshua) should not march and blow the ramhorn so the walls (of segregation) will not come tumbling down. See paragraph 31.

King, in paragraph 32, then makes his eleventh and final "let us" phrase." Whenever King begins to move upward to the climactic portion of the message, he speaks reality to his audience to ensure that they are fortified for the long-suffering, pain, and agony of the freedom struggle. Despite the reality of difficult days, King is announcing the completion of the process: from feet walking to moving (striding) to marching to victory, the triumphal march to the American Dream.

King knows that the issue of patience and waiting is critical to those who have suffered long, and he anticipates the questions of the audience: "If there is going to be more suffering, then for how long?" King finishes with his standard quotation from James Russell Lowell and asks one final time, "How long? Not long."

Then comes the final victory in the triumphant march to freedom. The metaphor connotes the marching of the civil rights movement, but now God is also marching. God is "trampling out the vintage where the grapes of wrath are stored" and "God's truth is marching on," and finally "Our God is marching on." In response to God's triumphant march, the civil rights marcher can only say, "Glory, hallelujah!" and "His truth is marching on." The process of victory at Selma is complete, and they continue the triumphal march to the American Dream.

Lessons for the Twenty-First-Century Struggle

The key to the fulfillment, expansion, and reclamation of the American Dream lies in the dissent of subjugated people for whom the American Dream was/is unfulfilled. King utilized the radical reformist jeremiad in "Our God Is Marching On" and gives us four critical lessons for those who engage in prophetic politics in the twenty-first century to reclaim the American Dream and dissent in any age.

First, similar to Adams in chapter 3, King is careful to locate evil in the American system. In King's estimation, it is not people who are evil, but the values of the system that establishes the behavior of people. Because people are not evil, King chose nonviolence to redeem people and avoided any opportunity to intentionally humiliate white people. As an example, when King states that segregation is on its deathbed, he does not mean that white people are on their deathbeds. For him, the only issue is how costly the funeral for segregation will be due to its defenders.[10]

The separation of an evil system from evil people is critical for the reclamation of the American Dream. Recently in a sermon, I offered a critique of the wide disparity in wealth and income of the few from the many and waxed eloquent about the massive uploading of wealth to one class of people since 1980. After the sermon, one gentleman walked up to me and said, "Based upon what you said, you want all the rich people and wealthy corporations to be taken out and shot." I said to the young man that I did not have hatred for the rich or wealthy corporations. I simply wanted people to recognize and admit that based upon the cumulative effect and ability of lobbyists, campaign contributions, and special-interest politics, the policies of this nation are slanted toward the rich and wealthy corporations, and if we want to save our nation, we must change this reality. It is important to communicate that we do not hate rich people or wealthy corporations. Our concerns are with the values of the system.

The second critical lesson is that King clearly demonstrates dangerous societal effects when the value of people is defined exclusively in a producer/consumer paradigm. When people are valued as consumers, or producers for that matter, rather than as human beings, the economic interests of the producers will dominate the nation. In paragraphs 9 to 13, based upon C. Vann Woodward's book *The Strange Career of Jim Crow,* King argues that racial segregation was based not in the hatred of races but in the financial interests of one class that positioned the poor white and the poor black against one another for profit and gain.[11] King suggests that for twenty years after the end of Reconstruction, southern states permitted biracial voting. The Populist party emerged with its voting alliance of "poor whites" and "Negroes," and this alliance was seen as a danger. Through the use of media control, bourbon interests campaigned for laws that criminalized whites and blacks coming together as equals. These laws crippled and destroyed the Populist movement of the nineteenth century. The threat of the united vote of blacks and whites resulted in the establishment of segregation to squash the threat of united white masses and Negro populations joining together to build the Great Society. The southern aristocracy took the world and gave the poor white man Jim Crow.

Of course, King implies that the civil rights movement is the new Populist movement and that white and blacks voting together can build the "Great Society."[12]

When people are defined as producers/consumers, then the system will confer the ritual of benefit to only 1 percent of the people, while the rest of the population—the middle class and the permanent underclass—languish. People have been separated across race, gender, sexual preference, class, neighborhood, and values to maintain the status quo of the ritual of benefit to a few. A new populism is needed to take back the interpretation of the American Dream from its economic stranglehold on this nation. Citizens, with a humane sense of values, can curb, guide, and control great business interests and the powers of government to the benefit of all the people. In the words of Langston Hughes from the Introduction: "O, let America be America again . . . The land where every man is free. The land that's mine—The poor man's, Indian's, Negro's, ME—who made America."[13]

The third lesson we can take from "Our God Is Marching On" is the inspiration that there have been significant shifts in the cultural myth of America based upon significant movements of protest. There have been points when the nation has lived up to its ideals and made a triumphal march to the American Dream. The second most frequently mentioned theme after "marching" in "Our God Is Marching On" is the affirmation of democratic ideals. King challenges the nation to rise to the democratic ideals it professes. By giving the Negro the right to vote, America put teeth into democratic ideals. It moved beyond the talk of freedom and into walking the walk of freedom. In paragraph 5, after discussing the Birmingham struggle and the fact that America's conscience began to "bleed," King says that because of Birmingham, the nation finally forced Congress to write the Civil Rights Act.

King pays respect to those Americans who cherish democratic traditions over ugly customs and privileges of generations and who come forth boldly to join hands with the civil rights movement. America acted on its stated ideals, and King calls Selma the most honorable moment in American history, when American people lived up to democratic ideals.

"Our God Is Marching On" is the most upbeat, hopeful, and optimistic speech of King's discourse. It is even more positive than the closing of the "I Have a Dream" speech because the optimism and hope of this speech is grounded in action: the extraordinary determination of blacks, whites, clergy, and people of goodwill from all over the nation to support the civil rights movement and equal voting rights for Negro citizens and the unprecedented decision of the president, Lyndon Johnson, to mobilize governmental apparatus to promote the civil rights agenda. In this atmosphere of victory and celebration, King advocates that all parties continue their triumphant march to the realization of the American Dream.

In paragraph 7, King praises President Johnson, who, in response to Selma, "generated the massive power to turn the whole nation to a new course." As we stated earlier, King even uses Johnson's phrase "Great Society" to describe what will happen when Negro and white masses unite. In paragraph 33, King says the goal is a society at peace with its conscience. A society that lives with its conscience is a society that rises up to follow its democratic ideals, and in Selma, America had lived up to its ideals. In celebration of this great victory, King tells the nation that America is on a triumphal march to the American Dream.

Finally, there is one more major idea expressed in the speech that dissenters of any age engaging in prophetic politics would do well to learn: King connects Selma with the cosmic battle of good versus evil. King does not ultimately base his confidence in democratic ideals, nonviolence, or marching. King's confidence is in God, and as such, King makes the battle over voting rights in Selma into a cosmic battle over eternal values. In paragraph 7, King calls Selma a confrontation between good and evil. Beginning in paragraph 25, the language comes from Joshua in biblical history, and the One who gives Joshua the victory is God (Joshua 6:20). The One who brings the walls tumbling down is God. From paragraphs 28 to 35, God is the guarantor of victory and therefore the prime mover. It is a cosmic battle between temporal and passing deceits and eternal values. The values become personified, that is, prejudice blinds, justice is crucified, and truth bears it. It is God who guarantees the death of lies, the raising of truth, and that justice will prevail. God ultimately rescues the eternal values of justice, truth, and freedom.

King moves beyond the secular poets and philosophers and goes right to the heart of the biblical tradition of the South when he concludes the speech by quoting "The Battle Hymn of the Republic": "Mine eyes have seen the glory of the coming of the Lord . . ." It is God who is marching on. King has already seen the victory (glory) of the Lord's coming—"His truth is marching on." In other words, when the civil rights workers are marching, God is marching. Each conflict with segregation is a conflict at the cosmic level with good and evil, and God must get involved. God is the guarantor that evil will never win at the cosmic level and never win at the material level in the struggle against segregation. The only appropriate human response is, "Glory, hallelujah! Glory hallelujah!"

Based upon prophetic politics the church critiques the values of the culture against the values of God. As I call for reclamation of the American Dream from its economic stranglehold on the nation, consider that God is not on the side of a few having and the vast majority of the people having not. The danger is that many movements that have harmed a great deal of people have claimed to have God on their side and that they represented God. The distinguishing factor of any movement that God sides with is the adoption of nonviolence. It is dangerous when we claim God and the means to the ends of God is violence, murder, and genocide. Nonviolent dissent is the key to reclaim the American Dream from its economic stranglehold on the nation.

Finally, King and Johnson are the two main actors on the American stage during the civil rights years: King, on the streets marching with direct action protests for freedom, and Johnson, in the halls of political power enlisting government to aid the ideals of equality. Johnson endorsed the movement by using the signature phrase, "We shall overcome." King endorsed Johnson's key social initiatives by using the phrase, "the Great Society." They both made voting rights for American Negroes a reality. On August 6, 1965, they met in the White House as Johnson signed into law the Voting Rights Act of 1965. Five days later, on August 11, 1965, riots broke out in the Watts neighborhood of Los Angeles, California. In 1965, Johnson began the escalation of American troops in Vietnam, often with little or no public fanfare. The urban riots and the Vietnam War would create new challenges for Johnson and King. Neither would ever be as hopeful and optimistic as their speeches of March 1965. Together, they changed the face of American democracy, but soon the partnership would be shattered and replaced by distrust and silence.

CHAPTER FIVE

PROPHETIC TRANSFORMATION: MARTIN LUTHER KING, JR., AND "BEYOND VIETNAM"

And we Americans are a peculiar, chosen people—the Israel of our time;
we bear the ark of the liberties of the world. . . . God has predestined,
mankind expects great things from our race and great things we feel in our souls. . . .
Long enough have we been skeptics with regards to ourselves, and doubted whether,
indeed, the political Messiah had come. But he has come in us.
—Herman Melville

The April 4, 1967, speech entitled "Beyond Vietnam" marked a fundamental line of demarcation in Martin Luther King, Jr.'s public ministry and positioned him on the fringe of American political discourse. King shifted his belief in the basic values of the American Dream and moved beyond the American jeremiad to a form of radical transformist dissent. King articulated structural flaws in the American system of democracy and free enterprise and sought radical transformation of American identity and values.

King's public discourse may be divided into two periods: 1954 to 1965, when King operated from the perspective of the radical reformist jeremiad, and 1966 to 1968, when King functioned as a radical transformist. To clarify the stark difference of King's discourse in the two periods, I compare "Our God Is Marching On" (1965) and "Beyond Vietnam" (1967). There are valuable lessons from this pivotal analysis of King's discourse for any contemporary movement of dissent.

"Our God Is Marching On" and "Beyond Vietnam"

As mentioned, King's radical reformist jeremiad in "Our God Is Marching On" is consistent with the tradition of the American jeremiad. It expresses a buoyant optimism and hope in the belief that the nation can overcome its unfulfilled values and continue the triumphant march to the American Dream. In contradistinction, King's radical transformist dissent in "Beyond Vietnam" is that of struggle and protest, not victory and deliverance. King is engaged in a fundamental critique of American identity and values that makes the tone of the speech deliberate and determined. Quite contrary to the affirmation and celebration in "Our God Is Marching On," King's speech argues that America is morally culpable in Vietnam and indicates that the culpability is related to structural flaws in the American system. King challenges the imperial aspects of the cultural myth of America and argues that Vietnam is not a matter of unfulfilled American values but a clear example of fundamental defects in the American system.

The radical transformist dissent and critique in "Beyond Vietnam" is clearly evident based upon subtle changes in tactical points of King's argument. For example, King maintains a commitment to nonviolence in both speeches, but in "Beyond Vietnam," the concept of nonviolence is used to critique America's reliance upon and determined commitment to violence. The value of nonviolence to peacefully solve problems is sharply contrasted with America's commitment to "using massive doses of violence to solve its problems" in Vietnam, even to the point that King accuses the American government of being "the greatest purveyor of violence in the world today."[1] In "Our God Is Marching On," King trumpeted nonviolence as the path to secure freedom and democratic ideals, and America accomplished democratic ideals through nonviolence; but in "Beyond Vietnam," King states that America has moved away from nonviolence, has committed itself to violence, and has moved away from the fundamental values of love, which for King is the essence of God's nature.

In another example of the shift in King's discourse, in "Our God Is Marching On," America is celebrated for its commitment to democratic ideals, but in "Beyond Vietnam," King highlights the glaring hypocrisy of America in that America professes democratic ideals at home but will not affirm and support democratic principles around the world. King states in "Beyond Vietnam" that when the Vietnamese people proclaimed their independence in 1945, and even "quoted the American Declaration of Independence in their own document of freedom, we refused to recognize them."[2] The lack of commitment to freedom and democratic ideals around the world illustrates America's true lack of commitment to freedom and democracy.

In both speeches King locates evil in the financial interests of one group over another. In "Our God Is Marching On," segregation is the result of the financial interests of one class that positioned the poor white and the poor black against one another for profit and gain. In "Beyond Vietnam," King situates evil in the financial interests of American capitalism over the interests of the poor of the world. Vietnam is evidence of a structural flaw in American capitalism based upon "pleasures that come from the immense profits of overseas investments."[3] According to King, as long as America is more interested in profits than people, "the giant triplets of racism, extreme materialism, and militarism are incapable of being conquered."[4] Clearly outside the jeremiad's perspective of change within the framework of celebration of the status quo, King calls for revolution, a "revolution of values," a commitment to people rather than machines, computers, property rights, and profit motives that can "save the soul of America."[5]

In "Our God Is Marching On," King identifies himself as an American citizen confident of American ideals, but in "Beyond Vietnam," he articulates another citizenship "beyond the calling of race or nation or creed" into a "vocation of sonship and brotherhood" that he calls being "a son of the living God."[6] King argues that the awarding of the Nobel Peace Prize is a calling that takes him "beyond national allegiances."[7] In "Beyond Vietnam," more than his identification with any race, nation, or creed, King positioned himself as a global citizen, particularly when any national or sectarian identification conflicted with his understanding of Christian love. King talks about his love for America and the fact that he is critiquing America as one of its citizens. But King constructs a higher citizenship that expands narrow loyalty to any one nation, particularly when that nation violates the precepts of God.

In the last example of King's shift, "Our God Is Marching On" closes with a cosmic triumph for God and an earthly triumph for protesters, whereas "Beyond Vietnam" closes with the future conditional and matters clearly left in the hands of human beings. In the closing of both speeches King quotes James Russell Lowell:

> Truth forever on the scaffold, (*Speak*)
> Wrong forever on the throne, (*Yes, sir*)
> Yet that scaffold sways the future, (*Yes, sir*)
> And, behind the dim unknown,
> Standeth God within the shadow,
> Keeping watch above his own.[8]

In "Our God Is Marching On," he quotes Lowell in the upward movement of improvisational celebration. The now classic "How long? Not long!" refrain is improvised and the Lowell quotation is improvised in the middle of the "How long? Not long!" King is in full celebration, fully expressing joy, affirmation, and hope. Yet, in "Beyond Vietnam," King does not appear to improvise in the closing stages of the discourse.

Listening to the audio tape of "Beyond Vietnam," I realize that the audience in New York is different than King's audience in Montgomery. In Montgomery, the audience is primarily southern African Americans who have just accomplished what many thought impossible, and they spontaneously use call and response to express their celebration. In New York City, the audience was primarily northern white Protestants, not hewn in the tradition of call and response, and moving against the tide of public opinion rather than riding the crest of victory. But I do not think the difference of audience explains the shift in King's nonimprovisational and celebrative style. King is operating as a social prophet who brings struggle, dissent, and protest, more in line with the European jeremiad than the American jeremiad. King challenges the cultural myth of America at its core,

54

and challenge is usually more deliberate than the spontaneity and emotion of celebration.

In "Beyond Vietnam," the concrete victory was ethereal and in the future, the date and time unknown, conditional upon human choice and decision. King says as the final words of the speech:

> And only if we will make the right choice, we will be able to transform this pending cosmic elegy into a creative psalm of peace. If we will make the right choice, we will be able to transform the jangling discords of our world into a beautiful symphony of brotherhood. If we will but make the right choice, we will be able to speed up the day, all over America and all over the world, when justice will roll down like waters, and righteousness like a mighty stream.[9]

In "Our God Is Marching On," the victory of the future is now, and Selma is a taste of more that is to come. In "Beyond Vietnam," there are days of long struggle ahead to convince the nation, and as a result the future is in human hands, "if only we will make the right choice."

The change in King's rhetoric from "Our God Is Marching On" to "Beyond Vietnam" is a shift from a radical reformist jeremiad to radical transformist dissent. This shift is based in King's movement away from belief in the basic values of the American Dream. In the early period of King's discourse (1954–65), consistent with the American jeremiad, King and the American public agreed upon four pivotal assumptions: (1) the American system is basically good, evidenced by the values of freedom, justice, and morality; (2) the American Dream is the most effective symbology for placing blacks in American society and for illustrating that whites and blacks are in the same universe of values; (3) faults in America, such as racism and segregation, are not indicative of systemic failure, but are rooted in unfulfilled values; and (4) acceptable protest is to participate in the American jeremiad, that is, the mainstream of American dissent (for instance, the abolitionists and progressive reformers), whose ideas and strategies for social change were a celebration of the values of the culture and of change within the status quo.

In the later period (1966–68), clearly evidenced in the "Beyond Vietnam" speech, King believed: (1) Americans and the Vietnamese are in the same universe of discourse, and inclusion and nonviolence are more effective than war; (2) based upon the use of violence, America is morally culpable in the Vietnam War; (3) Vietnam is more than a tragic mistake because it reveals a fundamentally flawed system of values; and (4) because the American system is flawed, there needs to be a radical restructuring of American priorities that King called a "revolution of values." As a result of this belief system, King could no longer sustain the idealism, optimism, and celebration of American values in the American jeremiad in the earlier period of 1954 to 1965. King jettisoned the American jeremiad and moved outside mainstream American political dissent. The jeremiad and its "celebration of change within the status quo" could not contain King's prophetic critique and dissent. King constructed an argument to persuade America of the need for radical transformation and change at the level of America's values. The response to the speech positioned King as a radically alienated social prophet.

In early 1967, King encountered William Pepper's photo essay "The Children of Vietnam" in *Ramparts* magazine. Many of the photos were graphic images of children burned by American napalm, and King decided to go public with his opposition to the war. Anticipating a deluge of opposition from President Johnson, the FBI, the American public, and the entire civil rights establishment, King and his staff carefully crafted his public speeches to minimize critique and resistance, starting with a speech in Los Angeles in February and Chicago in March. But the April 4 Riverside speech in New York City was the most carefully staged and served as his official statement on the Vietnam War. Though in some places it may seem redundant, I want to turn now to look at "Beyond Vietnam" itself.

"Beyond Vietnam"

Most critics agree that "Beyond Vietnam" has three critical thematic movements. The first movement of the speech begins with salutations and functions to build rapport and establish common ground with the audience. King reveals the angst of breaking his silence about Vietnam and labels it a most difficult mission:

> The truth of these words [silence is betrayal] is beyond doubt, but the mission to which they call us is a most difficult one. Even when pressed by the demands of inner truth, men do not easily assume the task of opposing their government's policy, especially in time of war. Nor does the human spirit move without great difficulty against all the apathy of conformist thought within one's own bosom and in the surrounding world. Moreover, when the issues at hand seem as perplexed as they often do in the case of this dreadful conflict, we are always on the verge of being mesmerized by uncertainty; but we must move on. . . . We must speak with all the humility that is appropriate to our limited vision, but we must speak.[10]

King names the calling to speak about Vietnam a "vocation of agony."[11] He acknowledges that "for the first time in the nation's history a significant number of religious leaders have chosen to move beyond the prophesying of smooth patriotism to the high ground of dissent," the difficulty of overcoming conformist thought in his own bosom, the mesmerizing complexity of the issues in Vietnam, and the fact that he speaks with the humility of limited vision, but he must speak. King is engaging in prophetic politics, and based upon "the mandates of conscience," he must speak.

From this humility, King quickly turns to respond to the many people questioning him about the wisdom of opposing the Vietnam War. In response, King states clearly and concisely his path from the Dexter Avenue Church in Montgomery, Alabama, in 1954 to the Riverside Church in New York City in 1967. King lists seven major reasons why he brought Vietnam into the field of his moral vision: (1) war is the enemy of the poor because it steals resources properly used to eradicate poverty; (2) America is sending the poor to die in war in disproportionately high numbers; (3) America is using massive doses of violence to solve its problems; (4) war is poisoning the soul of America; (5) the Nobel Peace Prize takes King beyond national allegiances; (6) the ministry of Jesus Christ extends peace to all people; and (7) King shares with all people the calling to be a "son of the living God," an allegiance that is beyond race, creed, and nation.

King closes this first movement and transitions to the second by acknowledging his privilege and burden to "speak for the weak, for the voiceless, for the victims of our nation, for those America calls 'enemy.'" King posits as his warrant the eternal nature of the brotherhood of all based upon his statement that "no document from human hands can make these people any less our brothers and sisters."[12] King gives a history lesson on Vietnam from the perspective of the "enemy." King interprets the history of the Vietnamese people from 1945 to 1947, from the initial French colonization and recolonization to American occupation and bombing, and argues that the Vietnamese people must see Americans as "strange liberators":

> What do the peasants think as we ally ourselves with the land-lords and as we refuse to put any action into our many words concerning land reform? What do they think as we test out our latest weapons on them, just as the Germans tested out new medicine and new tortures in the concentration camps of Europe? Where are the roots of the independent Vietnam we claim to be building? Is it among these voiceless ones? We have destroyed their two most cherished institutions: the family and the village. We have destroyed their land and their crops. We have cooperated in the crushing of—in the crushing of the nation's only noncommunist revolutionary political force, the unified Buddhist Church. We have supported the enemies of the peasants of Saigon. We have corrupted their women and children and killed their men. Now there is little left to build on, save bitterness.[13]

King then speaks for the National Liberation Front, the "VC" (Viet Cong), and the "Communist" and argues for compassion and nonviolence toward the enemy:

> Here is the true meaning and value of compassion and nonviolence, when it helps us to see the enemy's point of view, to hear his questions, to know his assessment of ourselves. For from his view we may indeed see the basic weaknesses of our own condition, and if we are mature, we may learn and grow and profit from the wisdom of brothers who are called the opposition.[14]

After giving voice to the voiceless and those who are called "enemy," King admits that he is deeply concerned with our troops as well. He says that America is "adding cynicism to the process of death, for they [American soldiers] must know after a short period there that none of the things we claim to be fighting for are really involved . . . we are on the side of the wealthy, and the secure, while we create a hell for the poor."[15] King quotes one of the great Buddhist leaders of Vietnam who says, "the image of America will never again be the image of revolution, freedom, and democracy, but the image of violence and militarism." King demands that the war cease:

> The world now demands a maturity of America that we may not be able to achieve. It demands that we admit that we have been wrong from the beginning of our adventure in Vietnam, that we have been detrimental to the life of the Vietnamese people. The situation is one in which we must be ready to turn sharply from our present ways. In order to atone for our sins and errors in Vietnam, we should take the initiative in bringing a halt to this tragic war.[16]

King then lists five concrete steps that America should take to begin to extricate itself from Vietnam and offers support for reparations for Vietnam:

> Part of our ongoing [*applause continues*], part of our ongoing commitment might well express itself in an offer to grant asylum to any Vietnamese who fears for his life under a new regime which included the Liberation Front. Then we must make what reparations we can for the damage we have done. We must provide the medical aid that is badly needed, making it available in this country if necessary.[17]

He calls for conscientious objection as an alternative for the young men and women eligible for military service. He encourages all ministers of draft age to give up their ministerial exemptions and seek status as conscientious objectors. King ends the second movement of the speech by calling for creative protest:

> These are the times for real choices and not false ones. We are at the moment when our lives must be placed on the line if our

nation is to survive its own folly. Every man of humane convictions must decide on the protest that best suits his convictions,
but we must all protest.[18]

In the third movement of the speech, King shifts definitively into
the category of radical transformist dissent. After calling for withdrawal
from Vietnam and all persons of humane convictions to creative protest, he makes a decisive, rhetorical turn:

> Now there is something seductively tempting about stopping
> there [call for withdrawal from Vietnam] and sending us all off on
> what in some circles has become a popular crusade against the war
> in Vietnam. I say we must enter that struggle, but I wish to go on
> now to say something even more disturbing. The war in Vietnam
> is but a symptom of a far deeper malady within the American
> spirit and if we ignore this sobering reality [*applause*], and if we ig-
> nore this sobering reality, we will find ourselves organizing "clergy
> and laymen concerned" committees for the next generation.[19]

King argues that if Americans ignore this malady within the American spirit, then succeeding generations will be forced to attend rallies
against wars like Vietnam. I believe King means that without significant and profound change in American life and policy, there is the
distinct possibility of protesting war for several generations beyond
Vietnam. If that is so, then there is a responsibility for sons and daughters of God to protest over and over again. Had King ended the speech
with the call for withdrawal, he would have been controversial, but
controversial in the reform tradition of mainstream American political
dissent—the jeremiad. But by moving the argument to the level of the
"deeper malady within the American spirit," he begins to move outside
of the jeremiad to radical transformist dissent.

King argues America's complicity in the root causes of national and
global racism, extreme materialism, and militarism is based upon America's need to "maintain social stability for our investment accounts."[20]
All over the globe, King says, people are revolting against old systems
of exploitation and oppression, and yet America is consistently on the
wrong side of the world revolution, siding time and time again with
the rich against the poor because of our refusal to "give up the privi-

leges and the pleasures that come from the immense profits of overseas investment."[21] The remedy is a call for a "revolution of values." America must shift from a "thing-oriented society to a person-oriented society." King says: "When machines and computers, profit motives and property rights are considered more important than people, the giant triplets of racism, extreme materialism, and militarism are incapable of being conquered."[22] King calls for transformation, a revolution of the values of American society.

King then defines the revolution of values. A true revolution of values will "look uneasily on the glaring contrast of poverty and wealth" between the West and other nations; it will eradicate war and says, "this way of settling difference is not just"; it will know that "a nation that spends more money on military defense than on programs of social uplift is approaching spiritual death." King believes that a revolution of values is the best and only defense against Communism. The world is in revolutionary times with "the shirtless and barefoot people rising up as never before, but America has lost its revolutionary spirit":

> It is a sad fact that because of comfort, complacency, a morbid fear of communism, and our proneness to adjust to injustice, the Western nations that initiated so much of the revolutionary spirit of the modern world have now become the arch anti-revolutionaries. This has driven many to feel that only Marxism has a revolutionary spirit. Therefore, communism is a judgment against our failure to make democracy real and follow through on the revolutions that we initiated. Our only hope today lies in our ability to recapture the revolutionary spirit and go out into a sometimes hostile world declaring eternal hostility to poverty, racism, and militarism.[23]

King explains that a revolution of values means that loyalties must become ecumenical rather than sectional. Human beings must develop an overriding loyalty to humankind as a whole in order to preserve the best in their individual societies. King calls it "an all-embracing and unconditional love for all mankind." For King, love forces us to be bound by allegiances that are broader and deeper than nationalism and that possess a different ethic than violence in regard to how one treats an enemy. King advocates a worldwide fellowship beyond race, class, nation, and religion that he calls "the sons [daughters] of the living God."[24] King, in one stroke, unifies the Hindu-Muslim-Christian-Jew-Buddhist into a worldwide fellowship based upon a universal value acceptable to all human beings, the ethic of love in 1 John 4:7-21 in the Christian Bible:

> This Hindu-Muslim-Christian-Jewish-Buddhist belief about ultimate reality is beautifully summed up in the first epistle of Saint John: Let us love one another, for love is God. And everyone that loveth is born of God and knoweth God. He that loveth not knoweth not God, for God is love. . . . If we love one another, God dwelleth in us and his love is perfected in us. Let us hope that this spirit will become the order of the day.[25]

King pulls the human family back from the "god of hate" or "bowing before the altar of retaliation."[26] Americans have a choice between "nonviolent coexistentence or violent coannihiliation." The hearers cannot procrastinate because it is possible to be too late. King makes his most urgent and pivotal call for action:

> Now let us begin. Now let us rededicate ourselves to the long and bitter, but beautiful, struggle for a new world. This is the calling of the sons of God, and our brothers wait eagerly for our response. Shall we say the odds are too great? Shall we tell them the struggle is too hard? Will our message be that the forces of American life militate against their arrival as full men, and we send our deepest regrets? Or will there be another message—of longing, of hope, of solidarity with their yearnings, of commitment to their cause, whatever the cost? The choice is ours, and though we might prefer it otherwise, we must choose in this crucial moment of human history.[27]

King quotes the inspirational words of James Russell Lowell, "Once to every man and nation comes a moment to decide," and closes the speech by quoting the prophet Amos in the Old Testament and centering the choice for the future squarely in human hands: "If we will but make the right choice, we will be able to speed up the day, all over America and all over the world, when justice will roll down like waters, and righteousness like a mighty stream."[28]

The Audience Response

After the speech itself, King was upbeat and positive because of feedback from the Riverside audience and the fact that he had finally taken a public moral position after remaining silent for two years. King lived his life in the center of criticism and controversy, but he was not prepared for the swift and negative press that presented an almost universal condemnation for "Beyond Vietnam." A barrage of negative editorials began immediately. The *Washington Post* dismissed the Riverside speech as "sheer inventions of unsupported fantasy" and declared that many who had respected King "would never again accord him the same confidence."[29] The *New York Times* stated that the speech was the attempted "fusing of two problems [civil rights and peace] that are distinct and separate. By driving them together King has done a disservice to both."[30] *Life* magazine considered that King went "beyond his personal right to dissent" when he advocated a plan that clearly amounted to "abject surrender in Vietnam." Much of his speech, the editorial went on, "was a demagogic slander that sounded like a script for Radio Hanoi."[31]

Even more dismaying and painful to King was the hostility of many blacks, especially black leadership, including some of his closest friends. Henry E. Darby and Margaret N. Rowley in their article "King on Vietnam and Beyond," provide a concise summary of King's lack of support amongst black leaders based upon their fear of King's antiwar stance:

> Well known civil rights leaders and other prominent blacks such as James Farmer, Director of the Congress of Racial Equality, Roy Wilkins of the National Association for the Advancement of Colored People, Whitney Young of the National Urban League, Ralph Bunche, former United Nations Undersecretary, Edmund Brooke, Senator from Massachusetts, Carl T. Rowan, newspaper columnist, Jackie Robinson, then Special Assistant on Community Affairs to Governor Rockefeller of New York, and some members of SCLC were fearful that King's opposition would result in a loss of support for the civil rights movement.[32]

The NAACP Board of Directors passed a resolution against what they saw in King's speech as an attempt to merge civil rights and antiwar movements.[33] Black journalist Carl T. Rowan, then of the *Washington Evening Star,* observed King's transformation from "the Montgomery boycott leader with an uncanny knack for saying the right things" into a person "who has very little sense of, or concern for, public relations and no tactical skill."[34] Longtime King associate Bayard Rustin advised that blacks shun the peace movement on the grounds that their immediate problems were "so vast and crushing that they have little time or energy to focus upon international crises."[35] King was wounded by the lack of support by blacks.

According to Taylor Branch, even some of King's closest advisers were not positive about the speech:

> Stanley Levison considered the speech itself an obstacle to public understanding. "I do not think it was a good expression of you," he bluntly advised, "but apparently you think it was." With his trademark directness, Levison called it unwise to focus on Vietnamese peasants rather than average American voters. "The speech was not balanced," he told King. It was too "advanced" to rally his constituency, and covered so many angles that reporters sidestepped his message by caricature and label.[36]

By this time, President Johnson and his administration were squarely hostile and negative toward King, and it was reported that "the President 'flushed with anger' when he read the wire-service summaries of 'Beyond Vietnam.' "[37] According to Bill Moyers, Johnson regarded King as a "naïve black preacher [who] was being manipulated by a Communist [Stanley Levison]."[38] J. Edgar Hoover stepped up surveillance and propaganda efforts and explained in a private communication to Johnson, "based on King's recent activities and public utterances, it is clear that he is an instrument in the hands of subversive forces seeking to undermine our nation."[39]

Many critics did not bother to engage King's argument in the speech itself, but several took King to task for the facts that he presented in the speech. King presented "facts" in the speech as self-evident, real, and obvious to every rational being, but Adam Fairclough makes clear that several audiences disputed King's facts:

King tended to ascribe racism to those who dismissed his views on Vietnam on the grounds that he lacked any expertise in foreign affairs. Yet, in truth he did lack such expertise and therefore blacks as well as whites drew attention to the oversimplifications and hyperboles that cropped up in his speeches on Vietnam. Was it accurate to describe Diem as one of the most vicious dictators of the modern time? Did the Viet Cong emerge spontaneously, independent of the North? Was it valid to argue that the National Liberation Front was a non-Communist body merely because the official Communists purported not to control it? Were the "vast majority" of the Vietnamese truly on the side of the Viet Cong? King might also be accused of applying the standard of nonviolence inconsistently. He applied nonviolence to American policy, but was silent on the violence, atrocities, and oppression that could be squarely laid at the door of North Vietnam.[40]

King was accused of ingratitude, attempting to conflate separate issues, lack of expertise, risking loss of support for civil rights, exaggeration of the effectiveness of nonviolence in international relations, and supporting Communists, which was to practice subversive and traitorous behavior.

Though the overwhelming majority response to "Beyond Vietnam" was negative, there were several positive reactions. An editorial in *Nation* defended King's decision to speak out against Vietnam: "He could not urge his people to practice nonviolence in the streets of American cities and condone violence in the jungle and rice paddies of Vietnam."[41] *Christian Century* praised King for standing against the "obvious inseparability of wasteful war in Vietnam and postponed poverty programs in the United States."[42] These publications joined a small chorus of minority voices who agreed with and supported King's position. However, although there were some segments of King's audience who were in agreement with King, his argument failed. The speech was not convincing to the overwhelming majority of the American audience.

The Failure of "Beyond Vietnam"

An analysis of the speech's failure reveals the starting point offered by King was very different from that acknowledged by many Americans.

For King, Vietnam was not just a tragic mistake but an indication of a defective and morally bankrupt capitalist system. The majority of Americans might have agreed that the system was not perfect, but they overwhelmingly rejected the suggestion that it was "defective" or "morally bankrupt." In fact, most of the American audience would have affirmed that the American system of free enterprise and democracy was the best in the world and among the greatest institutions and inventions in human history. In that era, and today as well, the American audience had/has a difficult time with the premise that America was/is morally corrupt. Americans were divided as to whether the war was a tragic mistake, but only a small minority were willing to accept King's notion of moral bankruptcy. King spoke counter to the cultural myth of America and found fundamental flaws in the values and ideals of America.

King's basic and fundamental problem was, according to Robert L. Ivie, that the American "public was simply unwilling to accept any such analysis that focused the guilt on their nation alone."[43] One wonders whether the "Beyond Vietnam" speech would have been more persuasive had King used metaphors that did not represent the United States as solely morally culpable. At the broader level, Ivie's insights raise the question of whether the American public can support any rhetoric that does not affirm the fundamental goodness of America at any time, and King, in the last year of his life, undisputedly challenged the fundamental goodness of America. One wonders if King knew exactly what he was doing. If one is a doctor offering medicine to a sick patient, then one might consider metaphors that have the best chance of being heard. Or, if there are times when one adopts the role and position of the radical prophet, regardless of the outcry, one must speak the truth of moral culpability. The prophet feels "righteous indignation" and must speak truth to power without regard for the consequences. In the latter stages of King's life, he adopted the role of radical prophet. King was interested in radical change, and the majority of the American public was not. King, the radical prophet, manifested a revolutionary value system, although the majority of the American public adopted a more conservative stance emphasizing the values of loyalty, fidelity, and solidarity to American values and uniqueness.

King's argument also potentially failed because the American audience possessed a different values hierarchy. In any argument, the speaker may have a different hierarchy of values, meaning the values may not be different between speaker and audience, but how each prioritizes the values is. King called for a revolution of values and believed that the revolution of values would result in the following in America:

> People would be more important than profits;
> the gap between rich and poor closed;
> the nation would choose peace over war;
> the nation would become ecumenical rather than sectional;
> the nation would be on the right side of world revolutions;
> the nation would adopt love and reject hate.[44]

The majority of the American audience did not regard profits as more important than people or oppose closing the gap between the rich and the poor, but they placed a higher value on the intersection of American democracy and free-market economy. The majority of Americans believed, as stated, in capitalism and its "mindset of economic striving deemed to be both demanded and blessed by God himself."[45] These norms of free-market enterprise functioned as the officially endorsed cultural myth of America (the American Dream), and the majority of Americans believed it, supported it, and had difficulty with King's argument.

For King, at the top of his values hierarchy was the brotherhood and sisterhood of all, and when one treated another as "enemy," one demeaned their brotherhood and sisterhood. For the American public, at the top of their values hierarchy was the preservation of the unique character of American freedom, democracy, and free-market economy—the preservation of American cultural identity. For the American public, an enemy was anyone who threatened these cherished values. Many Americans would be willing to kill or be killed to preserve these unique values. As a matter of fact, it is a presumption from the perspective of the majority of the American public that all rational beings make war on their enemies to sustain their way of life. This value was a presumption that was regarded as normal and taken for granted by the majority of the American public.

In the first chapter, I explained that the American jeremiad created an "ideological consensus" involving American exceptionalism. The American belief in "the errand in the wilderness" and the vision of "a city set up on a hill" were rhetorical strategies of cohesion, the mythology that held American society together, but also had imperialistic aspects in regard to its treatment of indigenous people, slaves, and others. What truly incited the critics to regard "Beyond Vietnam" as "ineradicably radical" was that King called on America to give up its concept of American uniqueness and exceptionalism. For King, one of the by-products of American uniqueness and exceptionalism was imperialism, an attitude that resulted in genocide, slavery, racism, and violence. "Beyond Vietnam" was unquestionably regarded as radical because King adopted the formidable rhetorical challenge of reshaping centuries of American identity and mythology. I will return again in the final section to discuss King and American exceptionalism.

Lessons for Our Struggle

As we prepare to reclaim the American Dream from its economic stranglehold on the American nation, critical lessons exposed in the analysis of "Beyond Vietnam" give sober pause, raise searching questions, and help dissent shape a rhetorical strategy for the American public. First, the American audience has a difficult time with the premise that America is morally corrupt and does not affirm any dissent that questions the fundamental goodness of America. Do we believe that the economic stranglehold is a matter of unfulfilled values and therefore we are doctors offering the medicine of the American jeremiad to a nation, in which case our challenge might be to develop the rhetorical strategies that might give America the best chance to take the medicine? Or do we believe the nation is morally culpable, feel righteous indignation, adopt the role of the radical transformist outside of the American jeremiad, and speak truth to power regardless of the outcry and the consequences? Or, is there some other way, a unique and different manner to dissent in this twenty-first century? Is there some third way?

Second, how do we account for the fact that in any debate or discussion with the American public, there is the possibility of the same values, but a different prioritizing of those values? For example, in response to "Beyond Vietnam," the majority of Americans did not regard profits as more important than people or oppose closing the gap between the rich and the poor, but they placed a higher value on the intersection of American democracy and free-market economy. How do you help someone reprioritize his or her values? The major challenge is the entrenchment of belief in the norms of democracy and free-market enterprise as the officially endorsed cultural myth of America. Americans deeply believe in capitalism and its "mindset of economic striving deemed to be both demanded and blessed by God himself."[46] Is it possible to dislodge this kind of entrenchment? For the American public, the top of the values hierarchy is the preservation of the unique character of American freedom, democracy, and free-market economy—the preservation of American cultural identity, such as rugged individualism, the Horatio Alger myth that anyone can become rich and a self-made man or woman, and America as land of material plenty. How does one separate American democracy from American free-market capitalism? How does one separate the human being from an exclusively producer/consumer identity, when this reality has been deeply ingrained? On the surface, it seems virtually impossible. And yet, there is also a tradition of dissent that is essential to the myth of America. America was founded in dissent related to the power structure of Europe, and dissent in America can never die. How much dissent can America tolerate against its own power structures? Is the reality of the Great Recession a game-changer such that new possibilities for dissent might be open as never before? Or is the Great Recession simply a small speed bump on the triumphal march to the American Dream that has no ultimate effect on the values of this nation?

There are no easy answers to these questions, and as we ponder them, let us look at the contemporary treatment of a prophet who, like King in "Beyond Vietnam," prophesied outside of the America jeremiad and was vilified and demonized just as King was. The demonization of Jeremiah Wright, Jr., is a function of the co-optation of dissent to the cultural myth of America.

CHAPTER SIX

PROPHETIC TRANSFORMATION: JEREMIAH A. WRIGHT, JR., AND THE AMERICAN DREAM

Being born here does not make you an American. I am not an American,
you are not an American. . . . All we've seen is hypocrisy!
We don't see any American Dream.
We've experienced only the American Nightmare!
—Malcolm X

On March 13, 2008, ABC's *Good Morning America* aired four short video clips of what they characterized as "controversial comments" by the Reverend Jeremiah Wright, Jr., pastor of the Trinity United Church of Christ in Chicago.[1] Wright, on the edge of retirement, had served Trinity for thirty-six years, and was the pastor of then–presidential candidate Barack Obama, who had been a member of the church for twenty years. *Good Morning America* framed the four clips with the question, "Could the reverend become a liability?" ABC reviewed more than a dozen of Wright's sermons offered for sale at the church and chose 156 words of text to feature that morning. After the initial *Good Morning America* report, an unprecedented and continuous loop of media sound bites recycling "incendiary" comments by Wright generated a firestorm that Edward Herman and David Peterson, in their article "Jeremiah Wright in the Propaganda System," characterized in the following manner: "The United States witnessed the most brazen demonization in its history of a person based upon his race, his creed, and his ties to a presidential candidate."[2] At its extraordinary height, the intensity of the media blitzkrieg to turn Wright into "an object of mass ridicule" forced Herman and Peterson to conclude:

> By now, the sermons, lectures, and commentaries of Jeremiah Wright quoted, reproduced, and discussed by other sources, ranging from broadcast and cable television and radio, to print and, of course, weblogs and the internet-based audio- and video-hosting platforms such as YouTube, have been so numerous that sheer scale alone makes it impossible to define where his allegedly "controversial" and "offensive" statements begin and where they end.[3]

The sum total of the media's characterization presented Wright as "drawing up his own idiosyncratic religious vision and deep feelings of racial resentment in order to deliver incendiary messages to his largely black congregation."[4] Based upon this media narrative, these questions were raised in the public discourse: did Obama agree with and condone Wright's message? How could Obama sit in Trinity Church for twenty years and not share some of Wright's "controversial" convictions?

The continuous loop of sound bites by Wright took him completely out of context and radically distorted his message. Obviously, the major interest and value of Wright's sermonic comments to the media were Obama's relationship with Wright and the potential to embarrass and discredit Obama. The comments also served to feed "the voracious twenty-four-hour-a-day media appetite" for "news," and as a result, the story "took on a life of its own."[5] I wonder if any person could withstand such intense and public scrutiny of sermons, articles, books, writings, speeches, and teachings, when spliced together in sound bites, severing one's message from its context.

Herman and Peterson argue for more sinister motives in the media's handling of Wright's sermons based upon the contrast of the handling of comments by the reverends John Hagee, Rod Parsley, and Pat Robertson, who were linked to the Republican presidential candidate John McCain: "The Wright episode provides an outstanding illustration of this country's racism, chauvinism, and political biases." Herman and Peterson produce factual documentation of the racial and political bias in the media:

> For the ninety-six-day period from February 27 through June 1, mentions of Wright's name in conjunction with Obama's outnumbered mentions of Hagee with McCain's 10.5 times to 1; they also outnumbered mentions of Parsley's with McCain's 40.2 times [See Table 1 below]. Remarkably, even the Reverend Louis Farrakhan's name turned up in conjunction with Obama's more frequently than did McCain's with Hagee's or Parsley's— although Obama had no connection with Farrakhan whatso-ever. The Project for Excellence in Journalism reports that at the apex of its coverage (April 28–May 4), the Wright-Obama relationship "counted for 42% of that week's campaign stories," while at its apex (May 19–25), the Hagee-McCain relationship "accounted for only 8%."[6]

Table 1

Differential coverage of the candidates, by religious figure, February 27–June 1[7]	
John McCain & Rod Parsley	153
John McCain & John Hagee	583
John McCain & Pat Robertson	138
Barack Obama & Jeremiah Wright	6,146
Barack Obama & Louis Farrakhan	798
Barack Obama & Michael Pfleger	187

These figures indicate the intensity of the media's obsessive and recurring fixation on Wright and his relationship to Obama in comparison to John McCain's relationship with Parsley, Hagee, and Robertson. Herman and Peterson also analyze the hostility and derogatory language used in reference to Wright that was seldom used for Hagee,

Parsley, and Robertson, including the use of the words *divisive* and *divisiveness* to characterize preachers associated with Barack Obama and Trinity but not those associated with McCain.

To ensure that readers understand the unprecedented media barrage, Herman and Peterson document the derogatory language from all sides of the political spectrum used in reference to Wright:

> From the jingoistic right the denunciations were unrestrained: "anti-American, racist rantings" (*National Review*); "venomous and paranoid" (Ron Kessler); "grievance-mongering preacher animated by the voracity of hate" (Michelle Malkin); "hate-filled, anti-American black nationalism" (Shelby Steele); "black hate speech" and "racist rants" (Charles Krauthammer), "anti-American black supremacist" (London *Times*), "fatuous clerical rantings," "black chauvinist rhetoric," "foaming pastor," "conceited old fanatic" (Christopher Hitchens); "stuck in a late-Sixties time warp" (Stanley Kurtz); among countless others like them.
>
> But these were often matched and sometimes surpassed by the language of liberals: "histrionics of a loony preacher from the South Side of Chicago" (Bob Herbert); "ranting" and "fire-breathing pastor" (Frank Rich); "race-baiting diatribe" (Cynthia Tucker); a "self-centered jerk" who believes "It's all about me" and whose "self-indulgent antics" belong on the *American Idol* television show (Rosa Brooks); the "jibberjabber from the crazy ex-minister" (Patricia Williams); "bigoted and paranoid rantings" (*New York Times*); "weirdness, wrath, insult, blowhardiness, vanity, paranoia, divisiveness and trouble" (Katha Pollitt). Last but not least, Barack Obama himself referred to Wright's "ridiculous propositions," "outrageous comments," "very different vision of America," as "divisive and destructive," "something that not only makes me angry but also saddens me."[8]

The condemnation of Wright, reminiscent of the condemnation of King after "Beyond Vietnam," indicates an agitation at the level of the core values of the nation.

Herman and Peterson conclude that the media firestorm around Wright is indicative of the fact that Americans "cannot stomach powerful criticisms of U.S. foreign policy and domestic inequalities and racism."[9] Every society has cultural myths, "flattering fictions," or "strategies of cohesion," and when one makes radical rhetorical moves outside of the cultural myth, then condemnation and demonization is often the response. Americans can only hear social critique in the orbit of the American jeremiad. The American jeremiad limits the political choices of the social critic and does not allow for assessments of structural flaws in America, and therefore functions as a discourse of social control.

In light of the overwhelming condemnation of King and Wright, when one rhetorically jettisons the American jeremiad, one calls into question American core values, initiates crisis, and threatens social harmony. The American jeremiad functions to invoke American core values for the purpose of overcoming crisis and maintaining social harmony. Wright articulated long-standing African American and minority grievances, making visible and plain structural flaws in America, such as racism, materialism, and militarism; and the anxiety and hostility toward him exploded, even from media that purports to be "objective," "professional," "neutral," and "fair and balanced."

"The Day of Jerusalem's Fall"

I am very familiar with one of the sermons Wright was most criticized for in the media, "The Day of Jerusalem's Fall," during which he allegedly blamed America for 9/11. I edited the sermon for a publication and believe the media's characterization of the sermon is an exaggerated and extreme caricature.[10] Many people who actually took the time to read the entire sermon in context had the experience of Rabbi Sharon Kleinbaum:

> Rabbi Kleinbaum sought out the complete texts of the [Wright] sermons in question, and discovered what you might expect: these clips were ripped out of context resulting in a totally distorted interpretation of them. What Rabbi Kleinbaum discovered were that these 45-minute sermons, being mischaracterized based on 30 second clips, were not anti-U.S. diatribes. They were deeply traditional, carefully composed and structured talks in the Biblical tradition of such venerated sources as Isaiah, Jeremiah, and Deuteronomy, one of the books of the Jewish scriptures. They were solidly in the tradition of the ancient prophets,

who would catalogue the sins of the people and invoke the Divine litany of curses upon people who have wandered from the righteous path prescribed in Scripture. . . .Wright did not preach a sermon condemning America, if one views the entire sermon and the contested portions in context. He preached a sermon pointing out the disconnect with our professed religious beliefs and the actions of our country. As a latter-day Jeremiah, he warned about the litany of objectionable things our country has done throughout our history, including recent history, and drew parallels from Biblical sources.[11]

As Rabbi Kleinbaum astutely observed, Wright's sermons were solidly in the biblical tradition of the ancient Hebrew prophets, who forthrightly addressed the sins of the people based upon their abandonment of their covenant relationship with God, and ultimately their judgment for "wandering from the prescribed path." Wright's sermons were outside the American jeremiad and harken back to the European form of the jeremiad. Wright's offense was his abandonment of the American jeremiad to express his social critique in the long-standing discourse of the Hebrew prophets and European jeremiad, disregarding American cultural optimism.

In response to the criticism that they took Wright's comments out of context, ABC published on their website excerpts from two of Wright's sermons as the "context." I would like to look closely at the two excerpts from Wright's sermons put forth by ABC:

The British government failed, the Russian government failed, the Japanese government failed, the German government failed, and the United States of America government, when it came to treating her citizens of Indian descent fairly, she failed. She put them on reservations. When it came to treating her citizens of Japanese descent fairly, she failed. She put them in internment prison camps. When it came to treating her citizens of African descent fairly, America failed. The government put them in chains. She put them on slave quarters, put them on auction blocks, put them in cotton fields, put them in inferior schools, put them in sub-standard housing, put them in scientific experiments, put them in the lowest paying jobs, put them outside the equal protection of the law, kept them out of their racist bastions of higher education, and locked them into positions of hopelessness and helplessness. The government gives them the drugs, builds bigger prisons, passes a three strike law, and then wants us to sing God Bless America . . . no, no, no.[12]

Not God bless America, God damn America. That's in the Bible, for killing innocent people. God damn America for treating her citizens as less than human. God damn America for as long as she acts like she is God and she is supreme. The United States government has failed the vast majority of her citizens of African descent. Think about this, think about this.[13]

Wright refuses the patriotic singing of the American jeremiad in song, "God Bless America," and evidences a lack of optimism about America's ability to change and calls for God's judgment, evidenced in the phrase "God damn America." Reminiscent of King, Wright criticizes America as an imperial superpower that rules the world by force and establishes its legitimacy by the mistreatment of people, including its own citizens, and especially African American people. Wright implies that America is still a racist society, the beneficiaries of the racism are still unwilling to change, and therefore America is damned. The litany of wrongs by the American government indicates an inability to change and therefore implies structural flaws in America and sets up the prospect of divine retribution. Wright's comments are in the tradition of the European jeremiad.

Wright also spoke within a tradition and lineage of African American social critique that lead to African-centered thought, what is known as Afrocentrism or Afrocentricity.[14] Initially, African Americans adopted the black jeremiad for their social critique of America, articulating the sin of slavery as the source of America's impending wrath from God. One component of the black jeremiad was black nationalism, and some black nationalists utilized the jeremiad in their critique. But many black nationalists held that America had already proven it did not include blacks, and therefore any future confidence in America was an illusion. These black nationalists shaped a separate black identity, adopting their own special mission and destiny for the black race, and utilized this cultural, economic, and religious myth as an alternative reality for the empowerment of African American people.

In the 1960s, black nationalism was central in ushering in a period of heightened religious, economic, cultural, and political nationalism that culminated in the Black Power movement of the late 1960s and '70s. Black nationalism also influenced Afrocentricity, which in most respects, is in direct opposition to the American jeremiad.[15]

For Wright, and many African-centered and black nationalist proponents, the jeremiad is a constricting form of social critique. The behavior of America toward African Americans does not warrant the optimism necessitated by the American jeremiad. The American jeremiad is openly dismissive of the grievances of African Americans, and directly ignores historical and contemporary white supremacy and white privilege. It is interesting that President Obama in his speech on race in Philadelphia on March 18, 2008, criticizes Wright on this very point, a lack of optimism about American's ability to change:

> The profound mistake of Reverend Wright's sermons is not that he spoke about racism in our society. It's that he spoke as if our society was static, as if no progress had been made, as if this country—a country that has made it possible for one of his own members to run for the highest office in the land and build a coalition of white and black, Latino, Asian, rich, poor, young and old—is still . . . bound to a tragic past. What we know, what we have seen, is that America can change. That is [the] true genius of this nation.[16]

Obama's criticism operates from within the optimism of the American jeremiad, but many African-centered thinkers and black nationalists do not have the confidence that America can change or can change fast enough to represent any real progress. Many in the black nationalism movement will assert that America's unwillingness to change is based in some sort of conspiratorial plot, often with the American government as the progenitor.

Some of Wright's critics dismiss accusations of media and racial bias based upon questions about the factual nature of some of Wright's claims. One statement that came under intense scrutiny was the truth claim in Wright's response to a question about the origin of AIDS. At the National Press Club, Wright was asked: "In your sermon, you said the government lied about inventing the AIDS virus as a means of genocide against people of color. So I ask you, do you honestly believe your statement and those words?"[17] Wright replied in part: "Based upon the Tuskegee experiment and based on what has happened to Africans in this country, I believe that our government is capable of doing anything."[18] Wright makes the AIDS claim in the midst of citing instances of the oppression of black people in America, including the Tuskegee experiment, during which the U.S. Public Health Service ran a forty-year experiment with six hundred black men who suffered with syphilis and were left untreated. Health officials followed the disease's progress in these men to their deaths and autopsies.[19] Notice Wright's response was not about whether or not he believed the truth claims in his statement, but his response was about the capability of the government. In Wright's view, based upon America's history of mistreatment of African American people, it is entirely possible that the government is capable of inventing AIDS as a means of genocide against people of color. The factual nature of the government inventing AIDS is secondary, and what is spotlighted is the dubious intent of government toward people of color. While the media debated the question of government invention of AIDS as to whether or not it is factually true, Wright is calling into question the fundamental goodness of America with respect to the treatment of African American people; he is questioning the myth of the American Dream based upon black grievance. Wright is suggesting the government is capable of a conspiracy against black people; and from Wright's perspective, only by ignoring the historical facts of the treatment of black people can one dismiss his claim, which, of course, is exactly what white power and white privilege does. The Tuskegee experiment is just such an instance of the conspiratorial intent of the American government.

Prophetic Indictment and the American Jeremiad

Part of the core problem of the demonization of Jeremiah Wright is that many highly educated and professional people in the media, and Americans in general, are unfamiliar with the rhetorical conventions of the American jeremiad. In support of this argument, M. Kathleen

Kaveny says: "the [Wright] controversy . . . demonstrates the relative unfamiliarity of Americans with the importance of the jeremiad more generally in the nation's political and religious history."[20] An example of this ignorance is the almost universal condemnation generated by Wright's aforementioned "God damn America" statement. Not one media pundit mentioned that philosopher, psychologist, and distinguished Harvard professor William James concluded one of his speeches by declaring "God damn the U.S. for its vile conduct in the Philippines."[21] James declared his opposition to America's pronouncement of sovereignty over the Philippines in 1898 and its decision to send American troops to war in the Philippines to enforce our declaration with massive bloodshed.

Richard E. Welch, in his book *Response to Imperialism*, records James's response to President McKinley's acquisition of the Philippines. James called it "the most incredible, unbelievable piece of sneak-thief turpitude that any nation ever practiced." Welch says:

> James believed that our war against the Filipinos was criminal. We had brought the Filipinos terror and destruction, in the guise of "benevolent" assimilation, and were guilty of "murdering another culture." By treating the Filipinos "as if they were a painted picture, an amount of mere matter in our way," we had fallen victim to the moral insensitivity of all conquerors who consumed weakness with inferiority and lost the ability to understand "the humanity of the enemy." "God damn the U.S. for its vile conduct in the Philippines."[22]

Intense debate and dialogue followed James's statement, but not the universal vilification and demonization heaped on Wright. In fact, Wright's statement mirrors James's pronouncement in that the mutual subject of both condemnations was America's mistreatment of innocent people. Herman and Peterson argue that Wright's critique of American foreign policy is central to the media attacks that he suffered:

> What is central is Wright's extensive and effective broadsides against U.S. and Western (or white European) policies and pretensions, including his criticism of the United States as an imperial superpower that rules the world by force, and robs the lesser

powers in order to maintain its great wealth, without concern for the people that it damages.[23]

Wright's critique of America sounds, in essence, exactly the same as James's critique. Reporters did a great deal of research in regard to the Wright story, but the glaring omission in their account was the historical rhetorical conventions of the American jeremiad.

As part of the nation's rhetorical conventions of the American jeremiad, important American religious figures have offered a similar challenge and critique as Wright has offered. Frank Schaeffer, son of religious right leader Francis Schaeffer, points out that when Wright criticized the government for racism and injustice, he was condemned, but when his father denounced America, and even called for the violent overthrow of the U.S. government, he was invited to lunch with presidents Ford, Reagan, and Bush, Sr. Schaeffer maintains that many right-wing white preachers denounce America's sins from tens of thousands of pulpits each Sunday. They attack America for tolerating "gays" like Sodom and Gomorrah, public schools for being against the Bible because they teach evolution, sex educators for corrupting youth and promoting promiscuity, and America for murdering the unborn on a regular basis in sanctioning abortion. Schaeffer says these right-wing white preachers contend, "as my dad often did, that we are, 'under the judgment of God.'" They call America evil and warn of immanent destruction. By comparison Obama's minister's shouted 'controversial' comments were mild."[24]

Schaeffer then, in line with Herman and Peterson's charge of racial bias, explicitly raised the question of race as the reason Wright was condemned:

> Take Dad's words and put them in the mouth of Obama's preacher (or in the mouth of any black American preacher) and people would be accusing that preacher of treason. Yet when we of the white Religious Right denounced America white conservative Americans and top political leaders, called our words "godly" and "prophetic" and a "call to repentance."[25]

First, Schaeffer's argument makes clear that many different groups utilize our nation's heritage of prophetic rhetoric and engage in prophetic politics. According to Kaveny, "Southern confederates used prophetic rhetoric as well as northern abolitionists; it was a tool of McCarthyites in the 1950's as well as anti-war activists in the 1960's."[26] Media pundits supplied no context that many on the Right and the Left use the nation's tradition of prophetic rhetoric.

Second, why was Wright's use of prophetic indictment labeled treason? Some, like Schaeffer, attribute it to American racism, while others, like Michael Eric Dyson, point to the lack of understanding of the black pulpit. From Dyson's perspective, white people are not familiar with the verbal intensity of the black pulpit:

> The black pulpit, historically, has been the freest place on earth for black people. When we could speak nowhere else, think nowhere else, talk nowhere else, and speak our minds nowhere else, the black pulpit was that forum. . . . The black pulpit has always been more than a mere station to distribute evangelical piety and theological truth. It has always, simultaneously been about expressing our hurts, our heartbreaks, our pains, the traumas, and the grief we had to endure. So, sometimes we had to get angry.[27]

Kaveny argues for another reason why Wright's comments are called treason: Americans are not familiar with prophetic indictments as a rhetorical form of the American jeremiad, and it leads to misunderstanding:

> . . . the phrase "God damn America" as used by Wright is undeniably shocking. It is meant to be. But it is also meant to call America to repentance and humility before God, not to call for her utter destruction. It is an oracle against Israel, in other words, not an oracle against the nations. In the vast majority of news accounts, however, it appeared to be closer in sentiment to an oracle against the nations, a fact which understandably would provoke a more intense reaction in those who heard it.[28]

According to Kaveny, prophetic indictments (1) demand that wayward citizens make a renewed commitment to the moral basis of their community and (2) shock wayward members of the community out of the indifference to their own flagrant pattern of sins and the harm those sins cause to other members of the community. She distinguishes two kinds of prophetic indictments found in the prophetic books of the Bible. First, "oracle[s] against the nations" are prophetic utterances in which God punished the nations, excluding Israel and Judah, for their sin, and the punishment often took the form of destruction and obliteration. Second, "oracle[s] against Israel and Judah" are different because God chastises God's people frequently in language as harsh as that of oracles against the nations, but God repeatedly forgives. God often uses the nations to punish Israel and Judah, but in the end, God restores the people and the destruction is undone. Because of a lack of familiarity with the African American prophetic tradition, Wright's comments are heard as an oracle against the nations rather than as an oracle against Israel and Judah. Oracles against the nations are not designed to heal a political community and cannot be interpreted as constructive. They announce destruction and offer no hope of repentance and renewal. When the Puritans left Europe, as we mentioned in chapter 1, they articulated oracles against the nations in Europe. Wright's remarks were heard as destruction of the American community without any possibility of repentance.

It is important to note that from Kaveny's perspective, Wright is operating from within the American jeremiad. I counter that he was operating outside of the jeremiad; but despite this difference of opinion, her argument that behind the Wright controversy is America's ignorance of the rhetorical conventions of the American jeremiad and the prophetic preaching tradition of the black church is insightful and valid. She also has one more critical insight that helps us bring the American jeremiad to conscious reflection. She argues that prophetic indictments function as a type of "moral chemotherapy."

Kaveny argues that "all prophetic rhetoric, even prophetic rhetoric rooted in moral truth, has the potential to rip the moral fabric of the community to which it is addressed."[29] Prophetic indictment is strong and dangerous medicine for the body politic. When the human body suffers from the ravages of cancer, chemotherapy can be the hope for restoring health. At the same time chemotherapy can have destructive consequences and, if not administered properly, can do more harm than good and kill the patient. Kaveny says:

> So too with prophetic indictments, which I believe function as a type of *moral* chemotherapy. They can be absolutely necessary to preserve the fundamental moral fabric of the community. At the same time, they can rip a community apart, setting mother against son, sister against brother. This destructive potential is intimately connected with the inner logic of prophetic indictments; it arises from the way in which prophetic interventions affect the ongoing conversation. [30]

Kaveny suggests a helpful "rhetorical stance" for would-be prophets to take toward the community that they are addressing: (1) prophets should frame their remarks as oracles against Israel and Judah rather than as oracles against the nations; (2) prophets should stand with their audience in the trials and tribulations despite their sin; and (3) the prophets' calls to repentance are to be heard as constructive chastisement within horizons of hope and possibilities of community renewal. Kaveny's rhetorical stance is consistent with the central tenets of the American jeremiad. The media's characterization of Wright's comments as an oracle against the nations impeded any possibility of Wright's prophetic indictment being interpreted as operating from a helpful rhetorical stance.

The consummate danger and ultimate tragedy of the media's co-optation of Wright's prophetic indictment by sound-biting selected snippets of Wright's sermons is that the nuance, subtlety, complexity, and variety of Wright's ministry and thinking are lost to many hearers. Wright's helpful rhetorical stance in his prophetic indictment is lost to the nation. Wright's supporters characterize his prophetic politics as an oracle against Israel and Judah and constructive chastisement within horizons of hope and possibilities of community renewal. As a clear example, they cite Wright's presentation at the National Press Club on April 28, 2008. Wright made a thirty-nine-minute presentation before a spirited question-and-answer period. In the presentation, Wright made many statements that balanced and offered perspective to the media's sound-bite presentation and might even be considered to fit within the American jeremiad. Wright explained the media's sound bites as an attack, not on him, but "on the black church." Wright attempted to explain the unknown phenomenon of "the prophetic tradition of the black church," which has as its purpose liberation, transformation, and reconciliation. When speaking of the liberation ends of the prophetic tradition of the black church, Wright says:

> The prophetic tradition of the black church has its roots in Isaiah, the 61st chapter, where God says the prophet is to preach the gospel to the poor and to set at liberty those who are held captive. Liberating the captives also liberates those who are holding them captive. It frees the captive and it frees the captors. It frees the oppressed and it frees the oppressors. The prophetic theology of the black church during the days of chattel slavery was a theology of liberation. It was preached to set free those who were held in bondage, spiritually, psychologically and sometimes physically, and it was practiced to set the slaveholders free from the notion that they could define other human beings or confine a soul set free by the power of the gospel.[31]

When speaking of the transformation ends, Wright says:

> God's desire is for positive, meaningful and permanent change. God does not want one people seeing themselves as superior to other people. God does not want the powerless masses—the poor, the widows, the marginalized and those underserved by the powerful few—to stay locked into sick systems which treat some in the society as being more equal than others in that same society. God's desire is for positive change, transformation; real change, not cosmetic change, transformation; radical change or a change that makes a permanent difference, transformation. God's desire is for transformation, changed lives, changed minds, changed laws, changed social orders and changed hearts in a changed world. This principle of transformation is at the heart of the prophetic theology of the black church.[32]

And finally, when speaking of the reconciliation ends, Wright says:

> The black church's role in the fight for equality and justice from the 1700s up until 2008 has always had as its core the non-negotiable doctrine of reconciliation, children of God repenting for past sins against each other. Jim Wallis says America's racist

sin of racism has never even been confessed, much less repented for. Repenting for past sins against each other and being reconciled to one another—Jim Wallis is white, by the way—(laughter)—being reconciled to one another because of the love of God, who made all of us in God's image.[33]

Supporters of Wright argue that after his presentation, not one question was directed to him by any at the National Press Club that had anything to do with his presentation. The questions of clarification centered on the media's sound-bites narrative and are an example of the media creating a distorted, straw-man story and then asking a person to respond to their distorted story. The media constructed their own limited narrative of Jeremiah Wright to co-opt his message of prophetic politics, based on their limited understanding of the American jeremiad, lack of familiarity with black preaching, and the issues of race and racism unresolved in the cultural myth of America. The media ran with their version of the Jeremiah Wright story, regardless of the facts.

Admittedly, I have offered a pointed critique of the media in its characterization of Wright, but the question must be asked if Wright was complicit, or what did Wright contribute to diffuse or enflame the media controversy? Under the trying circumstances of almost universal condemnation, Wright exhibited restraint and was composed and knowledgeable in two different public presentations. In an hour-long interview with Bill Moyers on PBS, Wright detailed the history of the African American religious tradition and upended the outrageous caricature that most Americans saw in the avalanche of media sound-bite clips.[34] The second presentation was at the Detroit Chapter of the NAACP's Annual Freedom Fund Dinner, where Wright focused on the media's misrepresentation of the African American religious tradition.[35]

In a highly anticipated appearance at the National Press Club, Wright delivered a clear and insightful explanation of "the unknown phenomenon of the black church," but in the question-and-answer session, Wright's mood and tenor changed. Amy Sullivan Washington, in her article "Jeremiah Wright Goes to War," sums up the media's perspective on Wright's disposition in the question-and-answer period:

> But while Wright is a theologian, a teacher and a pastor, he is ultimately a performer. In front of a cheering crowd of supporters . . . he gave into temptation and lustily went after his critics. As soon as the questions began, Wright transformed into a defiant, derisive figure, snapping one-liners at the unfortunate moderator tasked with reading the questions and stepping back with a grin on his face after each one, clearly enjoying himself.[36]

Wright performed an African American rhetorical form known as "playing the dozens," or "doin' the dozens." The "dozens" is a part of the African American oral tradition in which two males, and now females, compete in a head-to-head competition of "trash-talking." They take turns insulting or "crackin' " or "dissin' " on each other or their adversary's mother or other family members until one of them has no comeback. The object of the game is to bewilder and confound one's opponent with swift and skillful speech based on verbal dexterity. The dozens is a contest of personal power—of wit, self-control, verbal ability, mental agility, and mental toughness. Each putdown, each "snap," ups the ante. Defeat can be humiliating; but a skilled contender, win or lose, may gain respect. The dozens is one of the contributing elements in the development of hip-hop, especially the practice of battling.[37] Wright was playing the dozens. There is a line in the response to one of the questions at the National Press Club in which Wright clearly identifies the form:

> And why am I speaking out now? In our community, we have something called playing the dozens. If you think I'm going to let you talk about my mamma—(laughter)—and her religious tradition and my daddy and his religious tradition and my grandma, you got another thing coming (applause).[38]

Playing the dozens or "signifying" is an African American rhetorical form, what Thurman Garner and Carolyn Calloway-Thomas call "an example of what we find when African American voices are foregrounded for a Black presence."[39] Signifying as an African American rhetorical form has been explicated by many scholars as a rhetorical stance, as an attitude toward language, as a means of cultural self-definition, and as a critical means to explore the African American literary tradition.[40] Despite the scholarly discussion, it is tremendously difficult to define signifying. D. G. Myers, in an article about Henry Louis Gates's classic work on signifying, *The Signifying Monkey*, says:

> What is the concept of signifying? Gates notes that "few scholars have succeeded in defining it as a full concept," and although he devotes twenty-five pages to the effort, it must be owned that he is little more successful. Gates is best at gathering together other people's definitions. To signify, according to the jazz musician Mezz Mezzrow, is to "hint, to put on an act, boast, make a gesture." The novelist Zora Neale Hurston defines signifying as "a contest in hyperbole carried on for no other reason." In these conceptions, signifying sounds not too different from the traditional category of rhetoric known as "epideictic," a term used for a display piece, a speech the sole purpose of which is to put the orator's gifts on display (*epideixis*), and not with any practical intention. Yet to assimilate black signifying to the "Eurocentric" tradition of classical rhetoric is to lose "what we might think of as the discrete black difference." And so Gates takes pains to track the concept to Africa instead.[41]

In this instance, at the National Press Club, Wright used signifying as a rhetorical stance whose purpose was to empower cultural definition and to claim space for black presence. In the attempt to explain Wright's shift to the verbal confrontation of the question-and-answer session, supporters rightly estimate that it was the fact that after delivering a critical lecture on the history and traditions of the black church, the questions from the press were related, not to the lecture, but to the media's characterizations—as if Wright had not spoken at all.[42] The media's questions again rendered Wright invisible, and Wright utilized signifying as a rhetorical act in the question-and-answer period and, I believe, to indicate black presence. Wright's, as Amy Sullivan Washington says, "performance" was signifying to claim rhetorical space for black identity in the midst of the perception of hostile Eurocentric forces.

The problem for Wright was that this African American rhetorical form was a complete mystery to non-African Americans. Most of the media responded just as Amy Sullivan Washington responded, stating that Wright was a "defiant, derisive figure, snapping one-liners . . . and stepping back with a grin on his face after each one, clearly enjoying himself."[43] The question must be raised if it was a wise choice given the fact that it enflamed the controversy. Even some familiar with the African American rhetorical form of signifying questioned Wright's rhetorical choice based upon the fact that many media pundits used the performance to further justify the sound-bite characterizations of Wright.

Lessons for Our Struggle

Co-optation is the basic strategy of the American Dream to deal with its history of imperialism, violence, racism, slavery, genocide, and the conquest of indigenous people. Prophetic politics calls America to balance and resolve the fact that America has released more creative energy into the world than any modern nation and yet is also imperialistic and violent on an unparalleled scale and level. What are the lessons of the media's co-optation of Wright's prophetic message for our struggle to reclaim the American Dream?

First and foremost, the prophetic indictment of radical transformist dissent can rip the moral fabric of the community and is analogous to chemotherapy for the human body. Chemotherapy is strong medicine and can heal if handled properly; but if not handled properly, it can do more harm than good and can ultimately kill the patient. Prophets are doctors offering medicine to a nation, and prophets had better know that they are administering chemotherapy. To handle prophetic indictment properly prophets must (1) frame their message as "oracles against Judah and Israel," (2) stand with their audience in the trials and tribulations despite their sin, and (3) make their call to repentance in such a way that it can be heard as constructive chastisement within horizons of hope and possibilities of community renewal. Given the reality of the Wright media blitzkrieg, it is questionable whether in this age of sound bites—distributed through television, radio, print, weblogs, and Internet-based platforms—prophets can ensure that their message is heard as constructive chastisement, especially when the issue has the radioactive tension of race and racism in America. Based upon the inability of the cultural myth of America to resolve the long-standing tension of America's contribution of more creative energy than any other modern nation with America's unparalleled violence, racism, and imperialism, the American media, on behalf of the American nation, co-opted Wright's message in order to discredit the message and the messenger, in hopes that the tension the message creates would go away.

Wright's prophetic indictment of America violated mainstream America's sense of civility, even though much of what he said was absolutely true and, to millions of Americans, absolutely relevant. His mention of black grievance was perceived as "traitorous," "anti-American," and "black hate speech." Can black grievance outside of the American jeremiad be perceived as constructive chastisement? Or, consider: do African Americans make more social progress when they prophetically speak from the perspective of the traditional American jeremiad and its conservative values, rather than the radical reformist jeremiad or the radical transformist discourse of social critique? What may be needed is what many African Americans learned long ago and is best articulated by David A. Frank and Mark Lawrence McPhail in their analysis of African American speeches at the Democratic National Convention:

> While it may be noble and cathartic to speak unvarnished truths, reinforcing the values of those who already agree, African Americans have made the most progress when they have nested their politics and fate in multiracial movements, casting rhetorical visions designed to persuade a composite audience.[44]

In other words, have we moved to the place in America where the nation is not willing to address black grievance alone? Was Wright's chief fault a lack of mention of any grievances of white middle-class America? Must African Americans adopt a triumphant narrative of African American empowerment and liberation within the context of the American Dream? Despite the trauma of slavery, segregation, and racism, must African Americans demonstrate a commitment to bring America to its professed values of justice, freedom, and equality for all, in other words, operate solely from the purview of the American jeremiad? One narrative of America utilizes the American jeremiad and the other jettisons the jeremiad to express its social critique. Is there a third way? Let's turn now to Barack Obama, who seeks to bridge black and white grievance.

CHAPTER SEVEN

BARACK OBAMA AND THE MULTICULTURAL AMERICAN DREAM

*An "Oprah" persona whose life story as it is appropriated in popular
biographies resonates with and reinforces the ideology of the American Dream, implying
the accessibility of this dream to black Americans despite the structural economic and
political obstacles to achievement and survival posed in a racist society.*
—Dana L. Cloud

Based upon the inability of the cultural myth of America to resolve the long-standing tension of America's "twin dynamics of empire," the American media, on behalf of the American nation, co-opted Wright's message in order to discredit the messenger and the message, in hopes that the tension the message creates would go away. In the last several chapters, I have argued that many prophets engaged in prophetic politics are in a rhetorical dilemma as to whether the radical reformist jeremiad or radical transformist discourse is the best way to express social critique and deliver social change. The radical reformist jeremiad is not seen by some to be radical enough to express the depth of social critique and for others radical transformist dissent is not inclusive enough to cast rhetorical visions designed "to persuade a composite audience." As this book's purpose is the reclamation of the American Dream from its economic stranglehold on the nation, I must ask: is reclamation possible without "casting rhetorical visions to persuade a composite audience"? But how can you cast a vision for a composite audience

91

that does not resolve the dilemma of the twin dynamics of American empire and especially the historical and contemporary force of race in American life?

The election of Barack Obama as the forty-fourth president of the United States was the first time that the African American jeremiad built enough of a multiracial coalition to deliver an African American to the highest political office in the land. Obama, heavily influenced by first- and second-generation black immigrant discourse, adopted the African American jeremiad, molded it, and shaped it into a twenty-first-century multiracial narrative that was effective enough to win the 2008 presidential election. One of the key factors to his successful election was that Obama offered a compelling rhetorical vision and jeremiad for the nation that attempted to resolve the twin dynamics of American empire and the issue of race in America. The prime example of Obama's black immigrant African American jeremiad was his March 18, 2008, speech, "A More Perfect Union." In this chapter I carefully unfold the influence of Obama's black immigrant discourse on his African American jeremiad and then offer an analysis of this important speech.

Black Immigrant Discourse and the African American Jeremiad

In an article entitled "Black Like Barack," Joan Morgan raises the sensitive issue whether one has to be a descendant of American slaves to be identified as black or African American.[1] Morgan pinpoints the fact that 2,815,000 black immigrants from the Caribbean, Latin America, and Africa were living in the United States in 2005. These people tend to construct both a black and an African American identity. To highlight the magnitude of this number of black immigrants, Morgan, quoting the *New York Times,* suggests "that more people of African descent arrived in the United States voluntarily from 1990 to 2000 than the total who came as slaves prior to 1807, when the country outlawed the slave trade."[2] She argues that Obama's presidential run "forced all Americans to grapple with the fact that 'black' in America is a diverse, multiethnic, sometimes biracial, and often bicultural experience that can no longer be confined to the rich but limited prism of U.S. slavery and its historical aftermath."[3] Reflecting both the tension and the absurdities of race in America, during Obama's campaign, some blacks openly questioned whether Obama was, as he says in "A More Perfect Union," "black enough," while some whites questioned whether or not he was "too black." Morgan believes that Obama's precarious footing around the issue of race in the 2008 election cycle was caused less by Jeremiah Wright and more by the fact that Obama "complicates quite beautifully, not only existing constructs of race but all the traditional expectations, stereotypes, and explanations that we have come to expect from discussions around what it means to be black in America."[4] Obama is an American-born son of a black African father from Kenya and a white mother from Kansas. He is not black or African American in the sense that he was descended from West African slaves. Morgan raises the consciousness of and creates rhetorical space for a black African immigrant discourse that is "black and bicultural" in America, for which Obama is the poster child.

Morgan identifies several general characteristics of this first- and second-generation black immigrant discourse. She comments that black immigrants are often (a) more conservative in political ideology, (b) less likely to publicly embrace social programs like welfare, (c) stalwarts about black complicity in black conditions, and (d) have the strong conviction that racism is an undeniable reality, but not the ultimate determinant. Morgan offers her view of the perspective of many black immigrants:

> At our very core, we view America as a land of infinite possibilities because we know firsthand that it is possible to arrive in this country with nothing and build a life infinitely richer than the one that was left behind. We are in short, very up-from-the-bootstraps kind of people, a bit more Republican (although we tend not to vote that way), if not moderately Democratic, in nature than black leaders care to recognize.[5]

In the adoption of the Horatio Alger myth, Morgan, in explication of the sensibilities of black immigrants, goes as far as to share that some black immigrants hold the same prejudices about African Americans as working- and middle-class whites hold, that is, trumpeting the "laziness" of African Americans and the willingness of

African Americans to use racism as an excuse not to succeed in a land of obvious opportunity:

> And if we are to be unabashedly honest about it, some of us share the same prejudices about African Americans as working- and middle-class whites. The ones who, as Obama eloquently pointed out in his speech, "don't feel that they have been particularly privileged by their race. Their experience is the immigrant experience—as far as they're concerned, no one's handed them anything; they've built it from scratch."[6]

The immigrant experience is distinct from the African American experience, and many black immigrants who adopt a black or African American identity balance the belief of America as a land of opportunity with the caveat that opportunity has been restricted to African Americans because of race. This is the tightrope and tension that Obama is contending with in "A More Perfect Union."

Although there is a definite component of criticism of African Americans in Morgan's black immigrant discourse, there is also a tremendous amount of sympathy and solidarity with African Americans. Though they have not experienced chattel slavery, black immigrants often have experienced the painful legacy of colonialism, slavery, and imperialism. Many black immigrants and African Americans hold in common the pain and suffering caused by this second and imperialistic dynamic of American empire. Morgan argues against letting white people "off the hook" for racism and enlisting black immigrants in the project of painting a "post-racism" society by lauding the progress of black immigrants as "examples of the American dream and a direct indictment of the hopelessness of African Americans."[7] Morgan recognizes that four hundred years of slavery and the sanctioned inequalities of Jim Crow result in baggage that the black immigrant does not arrive with and as a result is able "to move faster and lighter on a vastly unequal American playing field."[8] In this vein of solidarity with the African American experience Morgan says:

> There are tremendous psychological and emotional advantages when you can sit in your American history class and not have your entry begin with the "stigma" of slavery. And then there is

not having to reach back as far as the vagueness of Africa, deny-ing the vastness of the continent and its own complicity in the transatlantic slave trade, to retrieve a meaningful connection to a land that fortifies your identity.[9]

She argues that racism has so "coded and corroded" African Ameri-can experiences in America that many African Americans, when presented with the candidacy of Barack Obama, believed that the pos-sibility of an African American president was remote and in the far distant future. But to black immigrants, an Obama victory was not unfathomable because black immigrants were taught to believe "that if you work hard enough in America, almost anything can happen."[10]

Although many black immigrants construct their identity as black or African American, Morgan argues that their experiences as immi-grants "in many ways makes us natural by-products of the American dream."[11] Again, Obama faces the tension of the immigrant experi-ence (America as land of opportunity) and the perception of the black experience (racism, slavery, segregation, and so on) as he stands as a second-generation black immigrant constructing an African American identity in the twenty-first century.

Barack Obama's "A More Perfect Union"

In the last chapter, I detailed the media firestorm surrounding the March 13, 2008, airing of sound bites from Jeremiah Wright. In response to the sound bites, and hoping to defuse the controversy, Barack Obama immediately distanced himself from Wright's remarks:

> Let me say at the outset that I vehemently disagree and strongly condemn the statements that have been the subject of this con-troversy. I categorically denounce any statement that disparages our great country or serves to divide us from our allies. I also believe that words that degrade individuals have no place in our public dialogue, whether it's on the campaign stump or in the pulpit. In sum, I reject outright the statements by Rev. Wright that are at issue.[12]

Despite these remarks, the controversy did not subside and continued only to escalate. Obama was forced to deliver a speech entitled "A More Perfect Union," on March 18, in Philadelphia, Pennsylvania. Reminiscent of John F. Kennedy's 1960 presidential campaign speech before Protestant leaders to address the issue of his Roman Catholic faith and the separation of church and state, Obama's address was highly anticipated and certain to be highly scrutinized. The issue for Obama was squarely race, with all of the tension and anxiety that race in America engenders. For many, failure in this speech could doom his presidential candidacy.

The racial divide was established by narratives resulting from different experiences in regard to the twin dynamics of American empire. When white Americans return to traditional formulations of the American jeremiad and highlight the dynamic of the unleashing of creative energies and trumpet American greatness in an unabashed patriotism, it pains many African Americans who were not included in American democracy, for example, when African Americans were defined as three-fifths of a person in the Constitution. When African Americans cite the other dynamic of the American empire, listing black and minority trauma and grievances, many whites, as Obama will later suggest of Wright, argue that African Americans are demeaning the goodness and the greatness of America. Traditionally, African Americans and white Americans argue about the historical and patriotic greatness of America. Obama joins his black immigrant experience with his identity as an African American and the African American jeremiad to attempt a resolution to this traditional American racial divide.

To highlight the fact that there was unquestionable greatness in the founding document of American democracy, the Constitution, Obama begins the speech quoting the famous opening words of the Constitution: "We the people, in order to form a more perfect union." These words are the thematic foundation of the speech and the main point that Obama will return to again and again. Obama celebrates the fact that the speech is set in Philadelphia, the place that "launched America's improbable experiment in democracy," and adopts America's immigrant narrative when he says: "Farmers and scholars, statesmen and patriots who had traveled across the ocean to escape tyranny and persecution finally made real their Declaration of Independence at a Philadelphia convention that lasted through the spring of 1787." Obama begins with the dynamic of the American empire that unleashes creative energies unsurpassed by any other modern nation.

Obama quickly shifts to the other dynamic of American empire that results in imperialism, slavery, racism, and genocide. Though the Declaration of Independence plants the remarkable idea of democracy, he suggests that the idea is "unfinished," and the perfection of democracy is in future generations. The flaw in the document, or "stain," as Obama suggests, was the "nation's original sin of slavery." The term *original sin* is a very strong metaphor as it compares America's stain of slavery to Adam and Eve's original sin in Genesis 3:1-7 that brought sin and its attendant evil and judgment into the human experience. Obama suggests America's sin of slavery is biblical and epic in proportion, and this is meant to balance Obama's trumpeting of the greatness of American democracy. Slavery divided the colonies and the 1787 Philadelphia convention until it was agreed to allow the slave trade to continue for at least twenty more years, leaving "any final resolution to future generations." The bedrock theme of Obama's speech is his conviction of the responsibility of each succeeding generation to perfect the union started by the founding fathers over time:

> The answer to the slavery question was already embedded within our Constitution—a Constitution that had at its very core the idea of equal citizenship under the law; a Constitution that promised its people liberty and justice, and a union that could be and should be perfected over time. And yet words on a parchment would not be enough to deliver slaves from bondage, or provide men and women of every color and creed their full rights and obligations as citizens of the United States. What would be needed were Americans in successive generations who were willing to do their part—through protests and struggles, on the streets and in the courts, through a civil war and civil disobedience, and always at great risk—to narrow the gap between the promise of our ideals and the reality of their time.[13]

Obama resolves the twin dynamics of American empire by shifting from a focus on past and traditional greatness to the perfection and completion of America's greatness at some point in the future by succeeding generations. In other words, rather than highlighting a static patriotic or oppressive past, Obama exhorts the nation to the accomplishment of the core ideals invoked in the Constitution as a work in progress to be completed by future generations. Each generation must do its part, but the fulfillment of the ideal will only happen in the future. Obama follows Abraham Lincoln, who also moved the perfection of the nation's core ideals to some future point.

In a series of debates with Stephen Douglass in 1858, Lincoln argues that the Declaration of Independence is not a static document with fixed truths completed in the past, but rather presents Americans with ideals as maxims, goals to be strived for that guide thought and action. Stephen Douglass argued against the equality of all human beings and contended that the Declaration of Independence did not apply to blacks. In the final debate in Alton, Illinois, Lincoln refuted this claim by making equality a maxim rather than a fixed truth.[14] For Lincoln, the Declaration of Independence sets forth general truths, rules of conduct, or fundamental principles such as equality that could be perfected only at some point in the future. Obama follows Lincoln's strategy and attempts to bridge American's racial divide. Following the force of logic of the African American jeremiad, Obama admits that the implementation of the founding ideal of America was flawed. Following the force of logic of black immigrant discourse, Obama admits that the ideal of American democracy is great and remarkable. Obama resolves this tension by suggesting that the design of America is to perfect the union in succeeding generations. Obama attempts to change the fixed narrative of racial discourse in America by suggesting that it is the responsibility of whites and blacks to perfect the union rather than to focus exclusively on white or black grievances and trauma.

Obama then connects his campaign for president with the long march of those who came before to perfect the union, which he describes as "a more just, more equal, more free, more caring, and more prosperous America."[15] Obama explains his justification for running for the presidency, which is to help the people of the American nation solve their problems together:

> I chose to run for the presidency at this moment in history because I believe deeply that we cannot solve the challenges of our time unless we solve them together—unless we perfect our union by understanding that we may have different stories, but we hold common hopes; that we may not look the same and we may not have come from the same place, but we all want to move in the same direction—towards a better future for our children and our grandchildren. This belief comes from my unyielding faith in the decency and generosity of the American people. But it also comes from my own American story.[16]

Obama believes that America can solve its problems together by the common understanding of the responsibility to perfect the union and the desire of all to provide a better future for our children and grandchildren. Obama believes in the perfection of the union based upon the decency and generosity of the American people and his personal American story.

Obama mentions that he is the son of a black man from Kenya and a white woman from Kansas. He has gone to some of the best schools and lived in one of the world's poorest nations. He married an African American woman and has family of every race and hue spread across three continents. He then endorses American exceptionalism: "I will never forget that in no other country on earth is my story even possible."[17] These comments are pivotal to the speech and are indicative of Obama's support of the Horatio Alger myth. The rhetorical force of this combined theme is found in the incorporation of black immigrant discourse and the African American jeremiad into the cultural myth of white Americans who endorse American exceptionalism and trace their lineage back to the *Mayflower*, including white minorities who immigrated to America in the eighteenth, nineteenth, and twentieth centuries. Obama embodies the unity and discourse that he proclaims to America in that his personal history and his genetic makeup model a nation that is more than the sum of its parts: "that out of many, we are truly one."[18] Obama is attempting to construct, from the African American jeremiad, a twenty-first-century multiracial narrative.

Obama comments that he noticed in the first year of his campaign that the American people were hungry for a message of unity. Despite the temptation to view his candidacy purely through race, he won convincing victories in majority-white states such as South Carolina, "where the confederate flag still flies," and even though "racial tensions bubble[d] to the surface."[19] Though some commentators identified him as "too black" or "not black enough," he was still able to build "a powerful coalition of African American and white Americans."[20] In light of the controversy over the Wright comments, he suggests that race was only "divisive" in the last couple of weeks of the campaign. He sets up the racial polarities of the political environment, indicative of the fixed racial discourse of America; on one end of the fixed racial discourse in America, some argue his candidacy is an exercise in affirmative action and the desire of liberals to "purchase racial reconciliation on the cheap," and on the other end, Jeremiah Wright, "who uses incendiary language to express views that have the potential not only to widen the racial divide, but views that denigrate both the greatness and the goodness of our nation and that rightly offend white and black alike."[21] He reminds the audience that he has already condemned in unequivocal terms Wright's controversial statements. He responds to lingering questions as to how he could sit in Trinity and hear Wright make controversial remarks by saying, "I'm sure many of you have heard remarks from your pastors, priests, or rabbis with which you strongly disagree."[22] But then he goes to the heart of his critique of Wright:

> But the remarks that have caused this recent firestorm weren't simply controversial. They weren't simply a religious leader's effort to speak out against perceived injustice. Instead, they expressed a profoundly distorted view of this country—a view that sees white racism as endemic, and that elevates what is wrong with America above all that we know is right with America; a view that sees the conflicts in the Middle East as rooted primarily in the actions of stalwart allies like Israel, instead of emanating from the perverse and hateful ideologies of radical Islam. As such, Reverend Wright's comments were not only wrong but divisive, divisive at a time when we need unity; racially charged at a time when we need to come together to solve a set of monumental problems: two wars, a terrorist threat . . .[23]

100

Obama's critique of Wright is that he has a "profoundly distorted" view of America that (1) sees white racism as endemic, (2) elevates what is wrong with America above what is right, (3) views the problems in the Middle East as rooted in Israel rather than in the hateful ideologies of radical Islam, and (4) speaks divisive comments when the nation needs unity to solve a set of monumental problems.

Alice Randall, in her article "Barack in the Dirty, Dirty, South," argues that Obama's use of the word *endemic* is the most important word in the speech.[24] She asks: "Is racism endemic to America, or a massive series of crimes that occurred in America?"[25] She believes Obama's comment that Wright "expressed a profoundly distorted view of this country, a view that sees racism as endemic," means that Obama asserts that racism is not endemic to America. Racism is an unfulfilled value rather than a structural flaw in the values of the nation. Obama's critique of Wright is grounded in the reformer tradition of the African American jeremiad and black immigrant discourse versus Wright's radical transformist worldview. Wright challenges American exceptionalism and racism as an endemic structural flaw in the values of the nation based upon the violent dynamic of American empire, while Obama sees the violent dynamics of empire as evidence of the nation's unfulfilled values.

Obama's multiracial narrative does not confront the nation's structural problems of race as Wright's discourse demands but de-emphasizes these issues that have the potential to divide and instead focuses on problems that Americans have in common such as terrorist threats, a failing economy, health care, and so on.

Continuing to offer a brief apologetic in response to the question as to why he sat in Trinity all those years, Obama gives a detailed discussion of the positive ethos of Trinity and Jeremiah Wright. He critiques the media's "caricatures" of Wright that are "being peddled by some commentators."[26] Obama notes that Wright helped introduce him to his Christian faith and the valuable ministry that Trinity has done in the community and he details his first experience at Trinity, set forth in his book *Dreams from My Father*. From Obama's perspective, Trinity is like most predominantly black churches that embody the black community in its entirety—the doctor and the welfare mom, the model

101

student and the gangbanger, raucous laughter and sometimes bawdy humor, and dancing, screaming, and shouting. He sums up his view of the black church when he says:

> The church contains in full the kindness and cruelty, the fierce intelligence and the shocking ignorance, the struggles and successes, the love and yes, the bitterness and bias that make up the black experience in America. And this helps explain, perhaps, my relationship with Reverend Wright. As imperfect as he may be, he has been like family to me. He strengthened my faith, officiated my wedding, and baptized my children. Not once in my conversations with him have I heard him talk about any ethnic group in derogatory terms, or treat whites with whom he interacted with anything but courtesy and respect. He contains within him the contradictions—the good and the bad—of the community that he has served diligently for so many years.[27]

And then the summation and conclusion of the Wright matter,

> I can no more disown him than I can disown the black community. I can no more disown him than I can disown my white grandmother . . . who on more than one occasion has uttered racial or ethnic stereotypes that make me cringe. These people are a part of me. And they are part of America, this country that I love.[28]

For Obama, his family, both his white grandmother and his black pastor, and the black community exhibit racial and ethnic stereotypes, but he loves them both and disowns neither. His family evidences the same racial and ethnic tensions as the American family. His family members are not to be dismissed, and neither are members of the American family. They are simply part of the union that must be perfected.

Obama then pivots from the defensive, in explaining his relationship with Trinity and Wright, to the offensive, in offering a solution to the race problem in America. Obama suggests that race cannot be ignored, because to do so would be to make the same mistake as Wright "to simplify and stereotype and amplify the negative to the point that it distorts reality."[29] The controversy of the Wright comments reveals the "complexities of race in this country that we've never really worked through, a part of our union that has not been made perfect."[30] If both parties walk away now, then America will never be able to solve challenges such as health care, education, and jobs. After quoting William Faulkner, who said, "The past isn't dead and buried. In fact, it isn't even past," he launches headlong into a pragmatic discussion of race.

The first order of business, from the perspective of the African American jeremiad, is to discuss the African American side of the complexities of race in America. He links many of the disparities that exist in the African American community today to inequalities suffered under slavery and Jim Crow. These disparities include:

> Legalized discrimination, where blacks were prevented, often through violence, from owning property, or loans were not granted to African-American business owners, or black home-owners could not access FHA mortgages, or blacks were excluded from unions, or the police force, or the fire department, meant that black families could not amass any meaningful wealth to bequeath to future generations. That history helps explain the wealth and income gap between blacks and whites and the concentrated pockets of poverty that persist in so many of today's urban and rural communities. A lack of economic opportunity among black men and the shame and frustration that came from not being able to provide for one's family contributed to the erosion of black families, a problem that welfare policies for many years may have worsened. And the lack of basic services in so many urban black neighborhoods—parks for kids to play in, police walking the beat, regular garbage pick-up, building code enforcement—all helped create a cycle of violence, blight, and neglect that continues to haunt us.[31]

Obama argues that these "memories of humiliation" haunt men and women of Wright's generation. Wright is part of a generation that has justifiable anger and bitterness as part of racial memory, and Obama suggests that even to this day, the anger, bitterness, fear, and doubt of mistreatment have not gone away. It does not often get expressed in front of whites but finds expression in barbershops, around kitchen tables, and occasionally, in sermons such as those offered by Jeremiah Wright on Sunday mornings. It is important to note that Obama locates Wright's views of America as a generational issue, one that Obama explains later can be overcome.

After explaining the African American side of the racial complexities of America, Obama, from the perspective of black immigrant discourse, or the African American jeremiad in private, critiques African American anger and suggests that it is not always productive and that it keeps blacks from solving real problems. The anger distracts African Americans by not allowing them to face their own complicity in their condition and to forge the multiracial coalitions and necessary alliances to bring about real change. Obama acknowledges that black anger is real and that to simply wish it away, or condemn it without understanding it, serves to widen the racial divide.

From the immigrant experience that is deeply rooted in the American jeremiad, Obama identifies a similar anger within the white community. He says that working- and middle-class white Americans don't feel privileged by their race:

> Their experience is the immigrant experience—as far as they're concerned, no one's handed them anything, they've built it from scratch. They've worked hard all their lives, many times only to see their jobs shipped overseas or their pension dumped after a lifetime of labor. They are anxious about their futures, and feel their dreams slipping away; in an era of stagnant wages and global competition, opportunity comes to be seen as a zero sum game, in which your dreams come at my expense. So when they are told to bus their children to a school across town; when they hear that an African American is getting an advantage in landing a good job or a spot in a good college because of an injustice that they themselves never committed; when they're told that their fears about crime in urban neighborhoods are somehow prejudiced, resentment builds over time.[32]

Like that of the African American community, this white anger is not expressed in "polite company," but it is ever present and visible and functions as a political force. It helped create the Reagan coalition (the Southern strategy), in which people angry over welfare and affirmative action shaped the political landscape in presidential politics for a generation.

Just as black anger is counterproductive, so is white anger, because it distracts white America from "the real culprits of the middle class squeeze: a corporate culture rife with inside dealing, questionable accounting practices, and short-term greed; a Washington dominated by lobbyists and special interests; economic policies that favor the few over the many."[33] Even in his analysis of the true culprits, Obama endorses the American dream. There are not structural flaws in capitalism, the American dream, or the Horatio Alger story, but the middle-class squeeze is the result of unfair dealings and practices based in short-term greed, in other words, unfulfilled American values rather than problems with the values themselves. Labeling the resentments of white Americans as misguided or racist has the effect of widening the "racial divide and blocks the path to understanding."[34]

Obama believes that black anger and white anger have helped distract both groups of Americans from the real issues, and as a result there has been a racial stalemate for years. Obama asserts hope and a firm conviction for a change in the deadlock:

> But I have asserted a firm conviction—a conviction rooted in my faith in God and my faith in the American people—that working together we can move beyond some of our old racial wounds, and that in fact we have no choice if we are to continue on the path of a more perfect union.[35]

Obama asserts that faith in God and faith in the American people working together will help all heal and move past racial wounds. Obama's optimism is indicative of his grounding in the American jeremiad. But it is not the American jeremiad of a return to traditional and patriotic greatness. Obama shifts the greatness of America to the future, in that it is our responsibility to perfect the union.

Obama lists practical steps to perfect the union. African Americans must "embrace the burdens of the past without becoming victims of the past." African Americans must: (1) continue to insist on justice in every aspect of American life; (2) bind their grievances to the grievances of all Americans (coalition building); and (3) take full responsibility for African Americans lives, for example, demanding more from our fathers such as spending time with their children and teaching them to never succumb to despair or cynicism and to believe that they can write their own destiny. Obama comments that the "quintessentially American—and, yes, conservative—notion of self-help found frequent expression in Reverend Wright's sermons."[36] But, according to Obama, Wright was in error because to embark on a program of self-help, a person must believe that society can change:

> The profound mistake of Reverend Wright's sermons is not that he spoke about racism in our society. It's that he spoke as if our society was static, as if no progress had been made, as if this country—a country that has made it possible for one of his own members to run for the highest office in the land and build a coalition of white and black, Latino, Asian, rich, poor, young and old—is still irrevocably bound to a tragic past. But what we know, what we have seen, is that America can change. That is [the] true genius of this nation. What we have already achieved gives us hope—the audacity to hope—for what we can and must achieve tomorrow.[37]

Notice again the joining of the Horatio Alger story (you can make it in America if you work hard) with the America-is-special story (only in America could one of the members of Trinity run for the highest office in the land). Grounded in the joining of black immigrant discourse and the African American jeremiad, Obama attempts to shift the discussion of race in America from the listing of grievances, anger, and the past to change in the present and future. Black and white can argue about the greatness of America from the perspective of one of the twin dynamics of the American empire, but the real task is to perfect the union or to work together for change in the future.

Obama then turns to white America to suggest how they can perfect the union. White Americans must acknowledge the legacy of discrimination, historical and current, and not just in words, but in deeds. Without the anticipated consequences of judgment, doom, and destruction, or an attempt to induce guilt in white Americans as a motivation to change, but based upon the responsibility to perfect the union, white Americans can (1) enforce civil rights laws,

(2) ensure fairness in the criminal justice system, and (3) provide ladders of opportunity not afforded previous generations of African Americans. These agenda items will help perfect the union, move Americans beyond the fixed racial discourse of generations past, and demonstrate that all Americans can work together to solve American problems: "It requires all Americans to realize that your dreams do not have to come at the expense of my dreams; that investing in the health, welfare, and education of black and brown and white children will ultimately help all of America prosper."[38]

Obama repositions the jeremiad from the lauding of traditional American greatness of the past to the perfection of the union in the future. White and black Americans can admit that the Constitution is both great and flawed. Both parties can release the attachment to grievances because perfection is in the present and future and not in the past. The founding idea of America is great, and it is our responsibility to work out the flaws and achieve a more perfect union. Obama supplies a warrant for the greatness of America by connecting the founding idea of America to the belief of all the world's great religions: "that we do unto others as we would have them do unto us" and "let us be our brother's [or sister's] keeper."[39] Obama paints a vision for Americans to find the "common stake we all have in each other, and let our politics reflect that spirit as well." Our common stake is a more perfect union exhibited by better health care and schools and jobs for all.

Obama then puts the choice out to the American public—either America can revert to old discussions and politics that "breed division and conflict and cynicism," or America can work on crumbling schools "that are stealing the futures of black children and white children and Asian children and Hispanic children and Native-American children."[40] Americans can solve the great "challenges of our time"— health care, employment, and housing concerns that plague the nation. This time, or rather, strongly and forcefully "Not this time," Obama asserts, Americans want to talk about the real issues rather than old stereotypes and racial politics:

> This time we want to talk about the shuttered mills that once provided a decent life for men and women of every race, and the homes for sale that once belonged to Americans from every

religion, every region, every walk of life. This time we want to talk about the fact that the real problem is not that someone who doesn't look like you might take your job; it's that the corporation you work for will ship it overseas for nothing more than a profit. This time we want to talk about the men and women of every color and creed who serve together, and fight together, and bleed together under the same proud flag. We want to talk about how to bring them home from a war that never should've been authorized and never should've been waged, and we want to talk about how we'll show our patriotism by caring for them, and their families, and giving them the benefits they have earned.[41]

This time Americans want to perfect the union:

I would not be running for President if I didn't believe with all my heart that this is what the vast majority of Americans want for this country. This union may never be perfect, but generation after generation has shown that it can always be perfected. And today, whenever I find myself feeling doubtful or cynical about this possibility, what gives me the most hope is the next generation—the young people whose attitudes and beliefs and openness to change have already made history in this election.[42]

Obama turns to the closing movement of the speech and does so with hope in the next generation. He clearly delineates the need for transformation in the older generation, as exemplified by Wright and his grandmother, and focuses on the future and hope of the next generation. He suggests that what cannot get perfected in the older generation, can get perfected in the next generation.

He tells the story of a twenty-three-year-old white woman named Ashley, who worked for his campaign in South Carolina. In a campaign meeting, she told her story. When she was nine years old, her mother contracted cancer, subsequently had to miss work, was let go, and lost her health care. Her mother filed for bankruptcy, and Ashley decided to help her mom. She convinced her mother to eat mustard and relish sandwiches because it was the cheapest way to eat. She decided to join the Obama campaign because she wanted to help millions of other children who also wanted to help their parents. Obama comments that Ashley could have gone the traditional way of cynicism and anger and could have thought that the source of her mother's problem was "that blacks who were on welfare were too lazy to work, or Hispanics coming into the country illegally." But Ashley decided to build coalitions and "seek allies in her fight against injustice."[43] Ashley finished her story, and the South Carolina campaign went around the room to hear stories of other participants. An elderly black man told why he was there. Obama says that the man did not bring up health care, the economy, education, or the war. He said, "I'm here because of Ashley." Obama quickly suggests that

> that single moment of recognition between that young white girl and that old black man is not enough. It is not enough to give health care to the sick, or jobs to the jobless, or education to our children. But it is where we start. It is where our union grows stronger. And as so many generations have come to realize over the course of the two-hundred and twenty-one years since a band of patriots signed that document right here in Philadelphia, that is where the perfection begins.[44]

Obama bridges racial and age barriers and puts hope in the younger generation to go out and redeem previous generations of the family. A young white girl engages an elderly black man to move beyond the racial wounds of the past. The next generation will perfect the union.

Of course, we do not miss the point that the next generation is working on the Obama campaign, which implies that his campaign and subsequent presidency will assist the next generation to perfect the union. After all, this is amongst other things a campaign speech to persuade voters.

Obama, heavily influenced by first- and second-generation black immigrant discourse, adopted the African American jeremiad, molded it, and shaped it into a twenty-first-century multiracial narrative. By combining American exceptionalism with the Horatio Alger story, and both with an African American reformist jeremiad, he attempts to inaugurate a new discussion of race in America: one that is centered not in the racial divisions of the past but in each American's responsibility to perfect the union. The American jeremiad locks in the racial past by setting perfection in the founding dream of the nation. Any critique of the perfection of the founding dream stirs anger and hostility in white America, while any mention of it as perfect stirs anger and resentment on the African American side. Obama breaks all of this down into the responsibility of both sides to work to perfect the union. Obama offers a variation of the African American jeremiad by involving black immigrant discourse and attempts to create a multiracial twenty-first-century discourse.

The Response to "A More Perfect Union"

The response to the Obama speech was positive in the mainstream media and general American public. It stemmed the tide on the dipping poll numbers amongst Independent voters that began at the initial airing of the Wright comments. Jonathan Alter of *Newsweek* said, "Barack Obama didn't simply touch the touchiest subject in America, he grabbed it and turned it over and examined it from several different angles and made it personal."[45] Tim Rutten called the speech "Obama's Lincoln Moment," comparing the speech to Abraham Lincoln's "House Divided" address, delivered upon his acceptance of a U.S. Senate nomination, which "changed the national conversation on slavery."[46] It propelled Lincoln's bid for the White House two years later. After Obama's successful presidential run, *The New Yorker* opined that the speech helped elect him President:

> In his Philadelphia speech of March 18, 2008, prompted by the firestorm over his former pastor, he treated the American people as adults capable of complex thinking—as his equals, you might say. But what made that speech special, what enabled it to save his candidacy, was its analytic power. It was not defensive. It did not overcompensate. In its combination of objectivity and empathy, it persuaded Americans of all colors that he understood them. In return, they have voted to make him their President.[47]

There were also media pundits who were not enamored with the speech. Syndicated columnist Charles Krauthammer dismissed Obama's speech as "a brilliant fraud" that failed to either properly pose or frankly answer the question of why someone who purports to transcend the anger of the past would remain in a congregation whose pastor epitomizes that anger, and he labels the speech an "elegantly crafted, brilliantly sophistic justification of that scandalous dereliction."[48] Despite several less than favorable comments, the speech defused the media-created firestorm over the Wright excerpts. The final word about the speech from the American public can be summed up in the comments by *Newsweek*:

> When he walked backstage at the Constitution museum, he found everyone in tears—his wife, his friends and his hardened campaign aides. Only Obama seemed cool and detached. The speech was "solid," he said, as his entourage, tough guys like Axelrod and former deputy attorney general Eric Holder, choked up. . . . While the Obamas and their aides were dining the night before, Marty Nesbitt, Obama's close friend and basketball buddy, called Obama on his cell phone and said, "Man, look, this is like a blessing in disguise." Obama held the phone away and said to the table, dryly, "Nesbitt says this is a blessing in disguise." On the other end, Nesbitt could hear the laughter. "Really," Nesbitt spluttered, "this is really a blessing in disguise." Obama replied, "Yeah, well . . ." and Nesbitt could hear more raucous laughter. But it was a blessing in disguise. Wright gave Obama a chance to deal directly with issues that had been the source of whispering or underhanded attacks in the lower precincts of politics, to take the high road on a matter of pressing national importance but on a subject that can be difficult to honestly discuss. He had shown calm good judgment.[49]

Out of this rhetorical crucible, Obama joined first- and second-generation black immigrant discourse with the African American jeremiad, shaped a twenty-first-century narrative that defused the controversy, and put his campaign to the presidency of the United States back on track.

Lessons for Our Struggle

Our purpose is the reclamation of the American Dream from its economic stranglehold on the nation, and earlier in this chapter we asked the question: is reclamation possible without "casting rhetorical visions to persuade a composite audience"? How can you cast a vision for a composite audience that does not resolve the dilemma of the twin dynamics of American empire, and especially the historical and contemporary force of race in American life? Obama offered a compelling rhetorical vision and African American jeremiad for the nation that attempted to resolve the twin dynamics of American empire and the issue of race in America. After three years of the presidency of Barack Obama, it is clear there is a vast difference between casting rhetorical visions during the campaign process and implementation of the rhetorical vision in the governance of the nation. I am not sure that America has adopted Obama's vision and become a postracial nation, and some even postulate that under Obama's presidency race relations have become worse. It might be that the complexities of the racial issue in America are such that they might never be resolved, or we will discover that Obama was correct and just ahead of his time.

Many Americans believe that America is a color-blind society, in which the problems of race and racism no longer exist. According to this line of reasoning, race was dealt with in the twentieth century when segregation was overcome, and the major social advancement African Americans have made since the end of segregation proves the point. There is no longer a need for protest movements and speeches against white oppression, because in the minds of many racism does not exist.

Geneva Smitherman offers more explanation and definition to the reality of America's perception of a color-blind society when she argues that the sociopolitical context of the black struggle is "decidedly different" in the twenty-first century because of the post–civil rights movement success of a black moneyed class: "There is now a sizeable, highly educated black middle and upper class. The NBA, the NFL, Hip Hop, and other forms of Black Popular Culture have contributed to the development of a bling-bling livin' large black elite with benjamins to burn."[50] In response to this new reality, Americans virtually erased concerns of social justice, poverty, and educational inequities from the American agenda. She even goes so far as to say that the "long standing genre of black protest oratory is all but dead in the twenty first century."[51] She specifically includes in her death pronouncement the prophetic discourse of the black church, except for the obligatory "occasional public talk by the Reverend Jesse Jackson on corporate responsibility to blacks, or the Reverend Al Sharpton on the shooting of some hapless young brotha by police."[52]

I believe that black protest oratory and the prophetic tradition of the black church are alive and well. First, both black protest oratory and the prophetic tradition of the black church exist independent of this new American reality regarding race and the media's reporting of black protest oratory and the prophetic tradition of the black church. Second, protest oratory and prophetic traditions of the black church are alive and well because numerous writers support and many writers have taken Obama to task for several of his arguments in "A More Perfect Union." For example, Adam Mansbach argues that it is very difficult to give moral equivalency to centuries of structural racism and white anger and resentment over affirmative action:

> Obama's insights about white anger were salient, but to characterize ire at affirmative action and at *the thought that others might think them prejudiced* as "similar" to the frustration by the victims of entrenched structural racism was disingenuous, and even irresponsible. I don't dispute that white resentments should be addressed, if only because white people will refuse to grapple with race unless they are allowed to centralize themselves. But to begin such a discussion—the mythic National Dialogue on Race—without acknowledging that structural racism is a cancer metastasizing through every aspect of American life is impossible.[53]

Obama suggests that "whites do not feel privileged by their race," but critics argue that there is a difference between feelings and objective realities. Despite how some white people feel, the objective reality in the historical past and the present moment is that there is white privilege. Mansbach argues that Obama's "soft-pedaling the reality of white privilege might help bring people to the table, but if they come under false pretenses, they will not stay."[54] Third, black protest oratory and the prophetic tradition of the black church is alive and well because this book is developed from, augments, and hopefully furthers black protest oratory and the prophetic tradition of the black church in the twenty-first century. Black protest oratory and the prophetic discourse of the black church are not dead.

I believe that the key to the fulfillment, expansion, and reclamation of the American Dream lies in the protest discourse of subjugated people, for whom the American Dream was/is unfulfilled. It might be that those of us excluded from the American Dream must cast our rhetorical vision to a composite audience and include issues of housing, health care, employment, education, and civil rights that affect all. Perhaps the Great Recession and the reality that so many have been excluded from the American Dream provide a new opportunity to cast another vision.

The third section explores Martin Luther King, Jr.'s concept of the Beloved Community, a vision releasing the genius of America without the domination and subjugation of people. Modeled on Jesus' concept of the reign of God, the section will challenge traditional understandings of American exceptionalism and offer practical insights that will help the reader reclaim the American Dream in this critical hour of our national life.

SECTION THREE

THE BELOVED COMMUNITY

The response to two cataclysmic events in the first ten years of the twenty-first century reveals the contemporary core values of American life. The first event occurred when al-Qaeda operatives launched planes into the World Trade Center and the Pentagon on September 11, 2001. Several days later, members of Congress strategized how to bolster consumer confidence and keep U.S. financial markets from tumbling. Representative Dick Gephardt, expressing the sentiments of President Bush and both Houses of Congress, said, "We've got to give people confidence to go back out and go to work, buy things, and go back to the stores—get ready for Thanksgiving, get ready for Christmas."[1] A week later, President Bush said, "Get down to Disney World in Florida. Take your families and enjoy life, the way we want to enjoy it."[2]

Andrew J. Bacevich labels the country's post-9/11 national security strategy the "Go to Disney World" approach.[3] Although financial stability is of critical importance, the "Go to Disney World" approach indicates a critical set of American values when, in the midst of one of the greatest national crises in the history of the country, the American citizen was asked merely to consume and enjoy life.

Americans were also asked to support the war on terror but were not required to actually do anything sacrificial. This is not to say that prayer, yellow ribbons, and acts of kindness toward American troops are not important acts of support, but we as citizens were not asked to give up anything to assist the war effort. The message was communicated: the government will handle everything. The war was described as global in scope and likely to last decades, but no effort was made to expand the armed forces. No additional revenue was sought to cover the costs of a protracted conflict. To fund the war on terror, Congress gave the administration all the money it wanted. Huge bipartisan majorities appropriated hundreds of billions of dollars, producing massive federal deficits and pushing the national debt from roughly $6 trillion in 2001 to just shy of $10 trillion in 2008. Many liberal Democrats who decried the war routinely voted to approve this spending, as did conservative Republicans who continued to trumpet their principled commitment to fiscal responsibility and balanced budgets. The nation's economic priorities went unchanged, and for the first time in American history, tax cuts were enacted in a time of war. So, as the American soldier fought, the American consumer binged, encouraged by American banks offering easy credit. The American people could have been asked to sacrifice. The only people who truly sacrificed were military soldiers and their families. Our consumerist response to this first major event of the twenty-first century is a prime indicator of contemporary American values.

The second major event in the first ten years of the twenty-first century was the Great Recession of 2007, the worst financial crisis since the Great Depression of the 1930s. It resulted in the collapse of large financial institutions, the bailout of banks by national governments, and downturns in stock markets around the world. In many areas, the housing market also suffered, resulting in numerous evictions and foreclosures, and it prolonged unemployment. It contributed to the failure of key businesses, declines in consumer wealth estimated in the trillions of U.S. dollars, and a significant decline in economic activity, leading to a severe global economic recession in 2008. The United States Senate, issuing the Levin–Coburn Report, found that "the crisis was not a natural disaster, but the result of high risk, complex financial products; undisclosed conflicts of interest; and the failure of regulators, the credit rating agencies, and the market itself to rein in the excesses of Wall Street."[4]

The average American citizen was asked to stand idly by and both sanction and stomach unprecedented fiscal stimulus, monetary policy, and institutional bailouts. Why wasn't the average American citizen asked to participate? Why weren't Americans asked to sacrifice anything? Rather than ask China to fund radically increased debt to bail out our economy, why wasn't the American citizen asked to sacrifice? Americans could have bought "hope bonds," what CNBC pundit Dylan Ratigan labeled as "bonds that people could buy that would give them a stake in whatever bank bailout money we had to spend."[5] This concept was modeled on war bonds that American citizens purchased during World War II to raise capital and help citizens feel involved in the war effort. Why didn't someone appeal to the average citizen's patriotism and conscience and ask for sacrifice for the good of the nation, rather than increase American debt to foreign lenders? Why is there no call for national sacrifice on everyone's part for the good of the country? Why are we asked to consume as if consumption is the answer to every calamity that strikes our nation?

The average citizen was not asked to participate, because American national values define citizens as consumers, and the argument is that the best thing for consumers to do in a time of crisis is to consume. In both of these cataclysmic crises, under both Republican and Democratic presidents, the American citizen was asked to be passive. The economic stranglehold that capitalism has on the American Dream has contributed to national values that foster a lack of sacrifice in American citizens. It seems sacrifice is anathema to American consumerist culture. If Americans sacrifice, then Americans will not consume, and if Americans do not consume, the economy will suffer, and if the economy suffers, then Americans will not have jobs. Americans must keep consuming at all costs.

To reclaim the American Dream from the economic stranglehold on the nation requires a redefinition of national values and the reconstitution of American identity, which means a redefinition of both the cultural myth of America and American exceptionalism. Next we briefly return to Martin Luther King, Jr.'s "Beyond Vietnam" speech to present an example of the monumental challenge of trying to change American communal identity by redefining American exceptionalism.

King and American Exceptionalism

James Jasinski rightly points out that when Martin Luther King, Jr., opposed President Johnson's prosecution of the Vietnam War in his "Beyond Vietnam" speech, King was in conflict with presidential war rhetoric that justified military action.[6] In order to garner support for war, President Johnson reconfigured the identity of the American audience because war demands a level of brutality that is normally considered immoral by most human beings. In convincing Americans of the necessity of war, Johnson reconfigured the identity of the American people into a "united community of virtuous warriors." Johnson reconfigured, and any president that goes to war reconfigures, the identity of the American public through presidential war rhetoric. Consider:

1. War rhetoric maintains a posture of absolute good versus absolute evil. We are absolutely good, fighting for truth, justice, democracy, and so on, while our enemy is absolutely evil and savage.

2. War rhetoric paradoxically must suspend the values it upholds. Because the enemy is absolutely evil and savage, the higher ideals that are being fought for (truth, justice, democracy, and so on) could never produce victory in a life and death struggle with such a savage enemy. Therefore, we must suspend our values, lest our enemy use them against us.

3. War rhetoric develops a narrative that explains why war is the only road to peace. The enemy's evil is presented, complete with numerous accounts of rebuffed attempts at peace and negotiation. The force of the logic becomes crystal clear that the only option is to quickly and summarily eradicate this evil by any means necessary.

4. War rhetoric indicates that at the conclusion of war and the defeat of evil there will be a higher moral order, that is, a future of freedom, peace, justice, and compassion. Victory in war is the vehicle to clarify national purpose and call the nation to a higher moral order.

Jasinski correctly postulates that King's task in opposing the war was not only "to dispute the expediency of military action, but also the burden of reconstituting communal identity."[7]

King's argument in "Beyond Vietnam" is that the only ethical response to the Vietnam War required an abandonment of American exceptionalism. The Vietnam War evidenced deeply disturbing levels of violence in the American character that were legitimated by America's cultural myths of an "errand in the wilderness," "a city set up on a hill," Manifest Destiny, the American Dream, and so on. The Vietnam War was indicative of an overcommitment to a capitalistic and free-market economy that led to "the giant triplets of racism, extreme materialism, and militarism." Blind to the dynamics of imperialism, America seemed to be on the wrong side of a world revolution. America initiated and supported violence against the poor all over the world.

The redemption of America required a "revolution of values," in essence, a new communal identity. Americans would have to reshape the cultural myth of America and the belief that Americans were unique, special, and different from the rest of the human family, and therefore could justify violence, genocide, and racism. Americans did not have the right to suspend eternal human values to serve American purposes in support of American notions of exceptionalism. Instead, Americans would come to understand that they were on equal footing and join the worldwide fellowship of the human family in which love of humankind trumps tribe, race, class, and nation. King sought to overcome imperialism as an aspect of the cultural myth of American identity. King's intent was not to destroy the cultural myth of America but to envision American exceptionalism without the justifications of the domination of subjugated people. King envisioned America without the negative side of the twin dynamics of empire, a nation without violence, racism, and genocide against subjected people.

King offered an alternative identity to the war based on a "united community of virtuous warriors." Rather than war rhetoric, King reconstructed American identity through articulation of a peace rhetoric based upon a worldwide fellowship of all people:

- King's peace rhetoric affirmed the basic "brotherhood" and "sisterhood" of the entire human family and functioned in direct opposition to the perception that any person or nation is absolute good or absolute evil. No one is savage.

- King's peace rhetoric opposed the temporary suspension of values to defeat the savage other. The higher ideals of truth, justice, democracy, and so on are eternal and will defeat the forces of evil on their own terms.

- King's peace rhetoric opposed a polarizing pro-war narrative and substituted a narrative of the history of violence and the damage of war as evidence that peace is our only option. King often coined this insight in the language of the choice of "non-violence or non-existence."

- King's peace rhetoric maintained that war could never lead ultimately to a peaceful end; that only peaceful means could ensure a peaceful end and lead us on the path of true human community and moral affirmation, the worldwide fellowship of all people.

Following the logic of King's peace rhetoric, to see the enemy as a fellow citizen was to obliterate the difference that constituted American identity in war. If they were no longer the noble savage, then who are Americans? King responded that Americans, like everybody else, are citizens and neighbors based upon being chosen and beloved of God. King attempted to shift the identity of America to participation in a worldwide fellowship that he called the "sons [and daughters] of the living God." The virtuous community required the abandonment of American exceptionalism and imperialism. All people—not only Americans, but all people—were chosen and beloved of God. King conceived an American identity without the domination of subjected people.

As suggested earlier, King's discourse in "Beyond Vietnam" evoked massive condemnation by American society at large. King's attempt at the reconceptualization of national identity was overwhelmingly rejected by the majority of the American public. The American public heard King's speech as a threat to the cultural myth of America and its strategies of cohesion. Therefore, King's speech was rejected, and King was positioned on the fringe of American discourse.

As we seek to reclaim the American Dream, our national values have reconfigured the identity of the American people into a "united community of virtuous consumers." Before we offer an alternative communal identity, one without the domination of subjected people, it is important to look carefully at how capitalist values came to dominate our national identity.

CHAPTER EIGHT

THE RISE OF
CAPITALIST VALUES

It is cold and we have no blankets. The little children are freezing to death.
My people, some of them, have run away to the hills and have no blankets,
no food. No one knows where they are—perhaps freezing to death. I want to
have time to look for my children, and see how many I can find.
Maybe I shall find them among the dead . . . I will fight no more forever.
—*Chief Joseph (1877)*

In 1877, the U.S. government, largely at the insistence of white set-
tlers who wanted the land, reneged on previous treaty commitments
and attempted to force Chief Joseph and the Nez Percé onto smaller
reservations in the Walla Walla Valley of Washington. General Oliver
O. Howard, on behalf of the U.S. government, threatened a cavalry
attack to coerce Joseph's band and other holdouts onto the reservation.
One group, led by Chief Joseph and the war chief Looking Glass,
refused. After some young warriors, enraged at the loss of their home-
land, staged a raid on nearby settlements and killed several whites,
the Nez Percé fled the area, heading east into Idaho, Wyoming, and
Montana in an attempt to reach Canada. They were pursued by General Howard, whom Joseph's band defeated in battle or consistently
outmaneuvered. The campaign, one of the most bloody and heroic
of the Indian wars, ended when Joseph and the remnants of his band
were finally surrounded by one of the three army commands that had
set out to intercept them. In blizzard conditions on October 5, 1877,
only forty miles from the Canadian border, Joseph met with the army's

commanders to surrender. His surrender speech, among the most famous speeches in American history, was written down by an army lieutenant:

> I am tired of fighting. Our chiefs are killed. Looking Glass is dead. . . . The old men are all dead. It is the young men who say, "Yes" or "No." He who led the young men [Olikut] is dead. It is cold, and we have no blankets. The little children are freezing to death. My people, some of them, have run away to the hills, and have no blankets, no food. No one knows where they are— perhaps freezing to death. I want to have time to look for my children, and see how many of them I can find. Maybe I shall find them among the dead. Hear me, my chiefs! I am tired. My heart is sick and sad. From where the sun now stands I will fight no more forever.[1]

America often, as in the case of Chief Joseph and the Nez Percé, appropriates revisionist history in regard to the role of indigenous people in American history. At Walt Disney World, Chief Joseph, in robot form, once again delivers his speech:

> Enough, enough of your words. Let your new dawn lead to the final sunset on my people's suffering. When I think of our condition, my heart is sick. I see men of my own race treated as outlaws, or shot down like animals. I pray that all of us may be brothers, with one country around us, and one government for all. From where the sun now stands, I will fight no more forever.[2]

There is a significant difference between the Disney version and the one recorded on the battlefield. Instead of being a result of an imperialistic land grab that resulted in freezing children, the death of the elderly, and a military campaign that ended only after the deaths of hundreds of American and Nez Percé soldiers, Chief Joseph's surrender speech has been turned by Disney into a testimonial to the cultural myth of America. Saying that America's "dawn" will lead to the "final sunset" of the suffering of the Indian people and "all of us may be brothers, with one country around us, and one government for all" is another example of the co-optation of dissent to minimize the effect of the negative side of the twin dynamics of American empire. In Disney's fictionalized version of the speech, Chief Joseph becomes a "true American" when it is understood that he wanted to fulfill rather than undermine the American Dream.

At Disney World, Chief Joseph supports the American Dream and adopts the tenets of capitalism. Richard H. Robbins argues that Disney bends history, and the future for that matter, in order to appropriate childhood "as a vehicle to encourage consumption at all ages and rationalize capitalism."Disney is "the conscious attempt to present the history of capitalism without the warts."[3]

The effect of Disney's presentation is to shape to a large extent how Americans view the world and make sure that they do not see parts of the world that are uncomfortable or disturbing, anything that would keep Americans from consuming. Robbins asks us to consider that something more than entertainment is going on—denial and consumerism.

Much of the economic stranglehold of capitalistic striving causes a masking, and even outright denial, of the negative side of the cultural myth of America, and the violence of capitalism in particular.

Capitalistic striving, encouraged by the arrival of the middle class after 1812, was heightened to a feverous pitch between 1880 and 1930, and as a result the values of the nation and the definition of a good and happy life changed dramatically. The producer/consumer paradigm of human nature became entrenched in American life, and the cultural myth of America facilitated the identity of the American as consumer. Robbins asks: how were the universe of the consumer and the consumer itself created? He argues that this was accomplished in four ways: a revolution in marketing and advertising, a restructuring of major societal institutions, a revolution in spiritual and intellectual values, and a reconfiguration of space and class.[4] As interesting and vital as all four categories are, because values and the reconstruction of American identity are at the heart of the reclamation of the American Dream from its economic stranglehold on the nation, I examine closely the revolution in spiritual and intellectual values.

The Transformation of Spiritual and Intellectual Values, 1880–1930

The culture of nineteenth-century America emphasized values of thrift, modesty, and moderation. Frugality and self-denial were the watchwords as 53 percent of the population lived and worked on farms and produced much of what they consumed. Household items were relatively simple and included a dinner table, wooden chairs, beds, and perhaps a carpet or rug. Americans did not have electricity, nor had the automobile been invented, and the money supply was limited.

Facilitated by a new therapeutic ethos, with an emphasis on the health professions and the popularity of psychology, along with the increasing autonomy and alienation felt by individuals as America ceased being a land of small towns and became increasingly urban, the culture shifted from frugality, moderation, and self-denial to periodic leisure, compulsive spending, ostentatious display, and individual ful-fillment.[5] There were four major factors that contributed to the trans-formation of these spiritual and intellectual values: advertising, credit, the radio, and mind-cure religion.

First, advertising was a revolutionary development in America that influenced the creation of the consumer. The goal of advertising was to shape consumer desires and create value in commodities by imbuing them with the power to transform the consumer into a more desir-able person. Rather than emphasize the nature of the product itself, advertisers began to emphasize the alleged effects of the product and its promise of a richer, fuller, life.

It was at this time that the idea of fashion arrived: "the stirring up of anxiety and restlessness over the possession of things that were not 'new' or 'up-to-date.'" Fashion pressured people to buy, not out of need, but for style. Advertisers pushed the idea that fashion made one a more desirable person.

Second, buying things on credit and going into debt has not always been acceptable in the United States. It was highly frowned upon in the nineteenth century. It was not fully socially acceptable until the 1920s, at which time it promoted the boom in both automobile and home buying. Credit is essential for economic growth and consumerism because it means that people, corporations, and governments can purchase goods and services with only a promise to pay for them at some future date. As we found out during the twenty-first century's recession, credit is absolutely critical to consumerism because the more credit that is available, the more people will consume.

Third, the radio inaugurated huge shifts in American life in terms of knowledge and mobility. Introduced in the 1930s, the radio spread quickly and widely. By the year 1934, 60 percent of American homes had access to radio, and within the next five years the number grew to an astounding 86 percent. Radios were also placed in cars, increasing their influence in American life. Americans listened to the radio 1 billion hours per week, and it became the preferred leisure activity. The radio increased Americans' knowledge of what was happening around the country or in foreign nations, and one of its most important roles in American life was as a primary vehicle for the spread of advertising and consumerism.

Finally, Robbins, following William James's *The Varieties of Religious Experience*, discusses the influence of "mind-cure religion," or what is known today as the power of positive thinking, expressed in late–nineteenth-century religions, New Thought, Unity, Christian Science, and Theosophy, among others. Mind-cure religion "maintained that people could simply, by an act of will and conviction, cure their own illnesses and create heaven on earth."[6] These movements were wish-oriented, optimistic, and sunny; the epitome of cheer and self-confidence; and completely lacking in anything resembling a tragic view of life. There was no sin, guilt, evil, darkness, duty, or self-denial, and only, as one mind curer said, "the sunlight of health." Salvation would occur in this life and not in the afterlife. God became a divine force, a healing power. These new religions made fashionable the idea that, in the world of goods and consumption, men and women could find a paradise free from pain and suffering.

Since 1930, it has become permissible to seek self-fulfillment in this life and find elements of satisfaction in manufactured commodities. The culture adopted the belief that the world is basically a good place where there is no poverty or injustice and inequities are only in the mind. By the 1930s, the consumer became well entrenched in the

United States, complete with a spiritual framework and an intellectual rationalization that glorified the continued consumption of commodities as personally fulfilling and economically desirable and a moral imperative that would end poverty and injustice.[7]

In terms of defining the good and happy life, the purpose of life is to consume. Technology is venerated because it produces things to consume, and therefore technology equals progress toward the good life. Progress is natural, and even American, because progress is the availability of consumer goods. Consumers must be shielded from the negative side of consumption. Nothing should distract consumers, because, even in the face of cataclysmic national calamities such as September 11, 2001, and the Great Recession, consumption creates the good and happy life.

By the end of the twentieth century, based upon even more sophisticated advertising and marketing, credit and debt instruments, and mind-cure religion distributed over massive cable and digital networks, the revolution of spiritual and intellectual values was complete. Moderation, self-denial, frugality, and savings gave over to unlimited consumption, ostentatious display, unfettered spending on luxuries, and compulsive shopping. The result was the Great Recession and the enduring reality that only 1 percent of America had access to the American Dream from the 1980s to the first decade in the twenty-first century. The Economic Policy Institute's 2011 briefing paper, "The State of Working America's Wealth," states:

> The Great Recession officially lasted from December 2007 through June 2009—the longest span of recession since the Great Depression. The recovery since then has proceeded on two tracks: one for typical families and workers, who continue to struggle against high rates of unemployment and continued foreclosures, and another track for the investor class and the wealthy, who have enjoyed significant gains in the stock market and benefited from record corporate profits. The Main Street–Wall Street divide remains as big as ever in the aftermath.[8]

To illustrate the wealth divide between Main Street and Wall Street with even greater clarity, consider a few statistics from the report:

- The destruction of wealth that resulted from the Great Recession was widespread but not uniform. From 2007 to 2009, average annualized household declines in wealth were 16 percent for the richest fifth of Americans and 25 percent for the remaining four-fifths.

- The divvying up of the total wealth pie, even as the pie shrank, was made more uneven due to larger drops in wealth for those at the bottom. The share of wealth held by the richest fifth of American households increased by 2.2 percentage points to 87.2 percent, while the remaining four-fifths gave up those 2.2 percentage points and held onto just 12.8 percent of all wealth.

- The wealthiest 1 percent of U.S. households had net worth that was 225 times greater than the median or typical household's net worth in 2009. This is the highest ratio on record.

- In 2009, approximately one in four U.S. households (25 percent) had zero or negative net worth, up from 18.6 percent in 2007. For black households the figure was about 40 percent.

- The median net worth of black households was $2,200 in 2009, the lowest ever recorded; the median among white households was $97,900.

These figures indicate the devastating effects of unlimited consumption, ostentatious display, unfettered spending on luxuries, and compulsive shopping on the average working family of America. Much as in the example of the purchases of designer shoe and purse consumption in chapter 3, for the most part, consumers have little, if any, wealth.

There is no innate desire in human beings to consume in order to be a more desirable person, and people were not born understanding that the purpose of life is to consume. Producers and advertisers create, encourage, and entrench this benefit in the cultural myth of America to the benefit of a select few.

There are those who do not agree with the argument of this chapter. The counterargument to my argument is that human beings, throughout history, have sought material luxury and that although over-consumption does indeed have its dark side, it has its light side as well, that "getting and spending have been the most passionate, and often the most imaginative, endeavors of modern life."[9] By emulating the consumption-driven lifestyle of capitalist culture, people around the world are being drawn closer together. In addition, some argue that "a rising tide lifts all boats," which is the Reagan "supply side" economic model that could through the majority of the twentieth century point to a rise in standards of living for all classes. Of course, the vast wealth and income disparity between the few and the many in the last thirty years, revealed by the Great Recession, sorely tests and disproves this economic model. The numbers reveal that only a few boats have risen.

My argument to these arguments is that there are indeed positive benefits to capitalism. As stated, capitalism participates in the twin dynamics of empire with positive benefits and negative consequences. But the negative consequence of capitalism outweighs the positive because the question must be asked: can the level of wealth enjoyed by a few also be enjoyed by all? And if we are able to attain such levels of wealth for all, what is the cost to the planet and environment? Can the planet sustain the level of material plenty if all participate in the benefits of a few? The answer to this question is that the planet cannot sustain this level of equality. Capitalism, or any other economic system for that matter, cannot deliver the benefits of a few to all. Capitalism cannot only deliver the benefit to a few at the cost of domination of subjected people. How do we articulate a vision of human living that does not include the subjugation and domination of others? How do we overcome the fundamental scarcity in material resources? This question is worthy of Jesus. The words of Jesus will help us reclaim the economic interpretation of the American Dream from its stranglehold on the nation.

CHAPTER NINE

THE BELOVED COMMUNITY

In my quest to release the economic interpretation of the American Dream from its stranglehold on the nation, I have outlined the true values underneath the cultural myth of America in the twenty-first century. What I have found is a profound shift from nineteenth-century values of frugality, thrift, moderation, and savings to twentieth-century values of ostentatious display, individualism, compulsive spending, and overleveraged debt. The result of this shift in values, culminating in the period of 1980 to the present, has been the accumulation of vast wealth for a very small few, while the overwhelming majority of the nation has struggled. The values beneath present wealth distribution illustrate that capitalism, or any other human economic system for that matter, cannot deliver the benefits of a few to all. The scarcity of material resources on the planet ensures that the level of wealth enjoyed by a few cannot be enjoyed by all.

What then becomes the principle of justification as to how a few can have so much and the others have so little? The cultural myth of America, "errand in the wilderness," "city set up on a hill," Manifest Destiny, the American Dream, and so on, become rituals of benefit to bestow value on some and exclusion on others. The result is the twin dynamics of American empire: the release of more creative energy than any other modern nation coinciding with unparalleled levels of violence, genocide, and domination of subjected people. How do we articulate a vision of human living that releases creative energy and yet

131

does not include the subjugation and domination of others? How do we overcome the fundamental human quandary of scarcity in resources and the conflict and violence that result from this reality? These questions are worthy of Jesus.

Since we are going to approach Jesus, let me be clear as to what we are asking Jesus: we are asking Jesus to resolve the fundamental human dilemma within the human family of the vulnerability of resources, and the conflict, war, violence, hate, oppression, racism, and genocide of civil, political, cultural, and economic systems that result from human attempts to resolve the dilemma. To further clarify the exact nature of the human dilemma and the resolution that we seek, I want to look at the paradigmatic story of Esau and Jacob in the Hebrew Bible.

The Story of Esau and Jacob

Admittedly, there is not time and space to adequately treat the biblical myth of Esau and Jacob in great detail. The term *myth* does not make any assumptions of veracity. Rather, it means stories, legends, or explanations from the worldview of a particular people that serve to explain practices, beliefs, historical events, and even natural phenomena.[1] According to Claus Westermann, the myth is a paradigmatic example of conflict between brothers in the human family:

> . . . conflict among brothers living together arises out of the family as the basic form of community. . . . Conflicts are part of human coexistence in all areas. This is unfolded in the narrative about Jacob and Esau. It serves as a corrective to that understanding of brotherhood which one-sidedly idealizes it as something qualified only by mutual love; but this is not truly biblical. In both the Old Testament and the New brotherly existence is characterized by the responsibility which arises out of belonging together, but just as much by the affirmation and prosecution of conflict.[2]

This quotation carries many assertions about human reality.

Westermann argues that in the primeval myth human beings were created for community (Gen. 2), that conflict is a part of brotherly

132

existence (Gen. 4), and that tension is part of the relationship between children and parents (Gen. 9). These very basic relationships in human community become the focus of the narrative in the patriarchal story in Genesis chapters 12–50: the relationship of parents to children in the Abrahamic narrative (Gen. 12–25), of brother to brother in the Esau-Jacob narrative (Gen. 25–36), and several family members to one another in the Joseph narrative (Gen. 37–50).

Though the focus is Esau-Jacob, these three narratives (Abraham, Esau-Jacob, and Joseph) took place in the context of the family unit expanding to tribes, and the tribal unit becoming a people and nation-state. According to Westermann, these three narratives illustrate "that whatever happens in these more developed communities and their spheres of endeavor, be it in politics, economics, civilization, education, art, and religion, goes back to whatever happened in the family. No form of community can replace the family."[3]

What happened to Esau and Jacob in their family continues to happen to generations of human families, and what happens to generations of human families, according to the Hebrew writer, cannot be spoken of without speaking of God. The sum total of the Esau-Jacob narrative is that family as family and the relationships of the family are based on God's action and also preserved by God's action. In a time of crisis, salvation is experienced as salvation by God. God establishes the values of the family such that "the vertical succession of generations is based on blessing; horizontal communal life is based on peace."[4] And even when human beings make war and violence, as is so often the case, and lose the ideas of the succession of generation by blessing and communal life based on peace, in the mind of the Hebrew writer, God will restore the family and human community.

The conflict between Jacob and Esau forms one narrative. It is prepared for in the introduction, during which Isaac and Rebekah give birth to two competing sons, Esau and Jacob (25:19-34); set in motion by the deception of Jacob over Isaac's blessing of Esau (27:1-40); rises to a climax in the murderous intent of Esau, the deceived one from whom the deceiver Jacob escapes by flight (27:41-45); and is resolved when Esau meets his brother, Jacob, on his return after a long absence and in changed circumstances, and they reconcile and live in blessing and peace (32–33). There is fundamental human drama between brothers in a family—deception and flight—and based upon God's activity, there is a return and reconciliation.

Rivalry and opposition are part of the coexistence of brothers in a family. The unalterable reason for it is that there are privileges and resources that are at the same time vulnerable. Family is the basic form of human community. Family involves responsibility to one another that can be named as mutual love. Conflict is also a part of the human family because, even in the context of mutual love, resources are vulnerable, meaning resources are sometimes scarce and not always enough to go around. Westermann suggests that we prefer the view of responsibility and mutual love as the idealized version of the family. This idealism is not true from the biblical perspective in the Old and New Testament, in which family is presented as responsibility and the prosecution of conflict.

When discussing Genesis 25:29-34, Westermann even goes a step further and interprets the conflict to be the result of two brothers embracing different occupations, or two forms of civilization:

> The reflective, clever, far-sighted younger one (the shepherd) over against the crude elder (the hunter) . . . the narrative is understood as portraying rivalry between two states; the aspiring shepherd speaks, triumphant and mocking, as he makes fun of the crude, clumsy, and stupid hunter. The shepherd by his planning and regularity has shown himself more capable of coming to terms with life. The older civilization of the hunter and gatherer, which once dominated the whole region, must withdraw into the wilds and lose significance.[5]

Westermann argues that what happens in the family happens in the nation and what happens in the nation happens in the family, which means the family rivalry extends to civilizations and economies all the way to modern time. Westermann gets at the heart of many human catastrophes:

> A phenomenon both important and well known in the history of civilization: aspiring, climbing status "puts down" the status it has suppressed. In a few strokes it sketches the drama;

the one who is growing economically strong despises the one who is waning. This is the root of many social disasters and conflicts.[6]

The family is the basic form of human community. With family members, there is responsibility arising out of belonging together and, because of limited resources, the affirmation and prosecution of conflict. We look now to Jesus to resolve the twin dynamics of empire as well as the dilemma of mutual love and the prosecution of violence that results in human catastrophe.

God's Government in the Human Heart

Jesus does not resolve the twin dynamics of empire based upon human values from the human realm. Jesus brings another reign and rule with an entirely different set of values and priorities. Jesus supplants our Esau-Jacob and twin dynamics of empire dilemma because our dilemma is from the perspective of human rule and Jesus definitively upends and supplants human rule with the reign of God, or what is more commonly called in the biblical text, "the kingdom of God."

To avoid distraction from theological dispute, consider a few matters in regard to the kingdom of God. First, "the kingdom of God" is a translation of the Greek phrase *basileia tou theou*. Several scholars argue that the common translation of *basileia* as kingdom is problematic and prefer *kingship, kingly rule, reign, queen,* or *sovereignty*.[7] I prefer the terms *reign* and *reign of God* and will use them throughout our discussion, except when I am directly quoting a scriptural text.

Second, the Synoptic Gospels use several terms for the reign of God: Mark and Luke use *kingdom of God*; Matthew uses *kingdom of heaven, kingdom of God,* and *kingdom* with no qualifier. The Gospel writer John uses *kingdom of God* and *kingdom.* There are fine and subtle theological differences among these terms, but for our purposes, given the limits of time and space, I take them on the whole to mean the reign of God and I will use them as such.

Third, when Jesus announces the reign of God, it is difficult for us to understand what he means without having an understanding of eschatology in the Old Testament prophets. In its simplest form, eschatology is a branch of theology concerned with the final events in the history of the world or of humankind. At the highest levels of theological debate within the field of biblical scholarship, it is difficult to find common agreement on the meaning of the term *eschatology*. According to the biblical scholar Henning Graf Reventlow, however, there does exist a near consensus that the idea of an absolute end of the world is unknown in the Old Testament.[8] At its core, Old Testament prophetic eschatology is the belief in a new future in the world, in concrete time and history, with a period that is totally different from the present one. We are not talking about biblical apocalyptic literature, in which final mysteries and meanings of the end times are hidden from ordinary eyes. We are not talking about Armageddon or heavy and esoteric symbolism revealing the end only to those to whom the Spirit of God has given "eyes to see and ears to hear." Prophetic eschatology, in the traditions of Jeremiah and Isaiah, deals with transformation in concrete time and history of people, politics, governments, and nations in this world. What makes it eschatology is that the new future is the final one in that "it is impossible that a new change could follow upon it."[9] Reventlow suggests: "The present state of things and the present world order will suddenly come to an end and be superseded by another of an essentially different kind."[10] Dualism is a feature of Old Testament eschatology, but the change will be in two historical periods and not between two worlds. In regard to eschatology, popular culture has entrenched the model of an apocalypticism and millennialism, in which a natural world is violently overcome and overtaken by a supernatural one, and as a result the public misperceives the true nature of Old Testament prophetic eschatology.

The critical component of Old Testament prophetic eschatology is the messianic element. The Messiah ushers in and announces the new age. In the new age, peace and harmony rein, evidenced by harmony with animals, destruction of weapons, the disappearance of disobedience and apostasy, and nations coming to Jerusalem and living in peace. An excellent example of the Messiah and the new age is found in Isaiah 11:2-9:

The LORD's spirit will rest upon him,
> a spirit of wisdom and understanding,
> a spirit of planning and strength. . . .
He won't judge by appearances,
> nor decide by hearsay.
He will judge the needy
> with righteousness,
> and decide with equity
>> for those who suffer in the land. . . .
Righteousness will be
> the belt around his hips,
> and faithfulness
>> the belt around his waist.
The wolf will live with the lamb,
> and the leopard will lie down
>> with the young goat . . .
> and a little child will lead them . . .
A nursing child
> will play over the snake's hole;
> toddlers will reach
>> right over the serpent's den.
They won't harm or destroy
> anywhere on my hold mountain.
> The earth will surely be filled
>> with the knowledge of the LORD,
> just as the water covers the sea.

Ultimately, the change will not be because of the people's return to God and repentance, but will happen by the transforming act and power of God, often through the Messiah. Ultimately, the messianic idea is the prophetic hope of political freedom, moral perfection, and earthly (material) happiness to the people of Israel in their own land and to the whole human race.[11]

Jesus begins his earthly ministry announcing the fulfillment of messianic hopes and prophetic eschatology and inaugurates the reign of God. In Luke 4:18-21, Jesus' first public teaching, quoting the prophetic eschatology of Isaiah 61, he announces:

The Spirit of the Lord is upon me,
    because the Lord has anointed me.
He has sent me to preach good news to the poor,
    to proclaim release to the prisoners
    and recovery of sight to the blind,
    to liberate the oppressed,
    and to proclaim the year of the Lord's favor.

He rolled up the scroll, gave it back to the synagogue assistant, and sat down. Every eye in the synagogue was fixed on him. He began to explain to them, "Today, this scripture has been fulfilled just as you heard it."

In Mark 1:14, after John the Baptist is put in prison, Jesus goes into Galilee preaching "God's good news." Mark records that at the inaugural point of his ministry, Jesus announces, "Now is the time! Here comes God's kingdom!" (1:15). Matthew, also commenting that Jesus begins after John has been put in prison, says in 4:17: "Change your hearts and lives! Here comes the kingdom of heaven!" The Synoptic Gospels are in unity and harmony, and the central message and work of Jesus is to announce and inaugurate the reign of God. A few examples of Jesus' mention of the reign of God give the reader an even greater sense of the importance of the reign of God to Jesus:

Luke 4:43, 8:1: "I must preach the good news of God's kingdom in other cities too, for this is why I was sent." . . . Jesus traveled through the cities and villages, preaching and proclaiming the good news of God's kingdom.

Matthew 6:33: "Instead, desire first and foremost God's kingdom and God's righteousness, and all these things will be given to you as well."

John 3:5: "Jesus answered, 'I assure you, unless someone is born of water and the Spirit, it's not possible to enter God's kingdom.'"

Luke 17:20: "God's kingdom isn't coming with signs that are easily noticed. Nor will people say, 'Look, here it is!' or 'There it is!' Don't you see? God's kingdom is already among you."

Mark 10:23: "Looking around, Jesus said to his disciples, 'It will be very hard for the wealthy to enter God's kingdom!'"

John 18:36: "Jesus replied [to Pilate], 'My kingdom doesn't originate from this world. If it did, my guards would fight so that I wouldn't have been arrested by Jewish leaders. My kingdom isn't from here.'"

The reign of God is based in the paradoxical nature of God. The reign of God is preached and therefore inaugurated: it is here and yet on the way. Though it somehow is never fully realized, it is so profound and so real that cannot escape its claim. The reign of God is plain, as in the simple parables Jesus used to explain the reign of God; but also because of the simplicity of Jesus' parables, the reign of God is mysterious in unfathomable ways. Jesus gave many parables, but the parable about a valuable pearl in Matthew 13:45-46 will illustrate: "Again, the kingdom of heaven is like a merchant in search of fine pearls. When he found one very precious pearl, he went out and sold all that he owned and bought it." The meaning of the parable is simple, and yet when one considers what it means in its depths—to sell everything one has to possess the reign of God—then we understand how complex and mysterious parables are.

The church is the reign of God in its visible and fallible form; though the church is often fallible, it still inaugurates the reign of God in the world. The reign of God is a fellowship of love, peace, and joy and is the most beautiful reality that the world ever has known. But it is challenging. And it is demanding. And it is exacting. The reign of God affirms what is good, true, and just in every age, and it corrects and judges what is misguided, unjust, and wrong.

The reign of God is not simply over a country or a group of people, but over the whole of human history. The reign of God is not about a geographical country or a particular race or ethnicity. It does not settle on boundaries and divisions that human beings make. The reign of God is not about a sentimental vagueness that does not require anything of us except that we try to be "nice." The reign of God is not a national or a political kingdom, but a community in God's care that lives in love, joy, peace, and righteousness. I heard this said once, and I have never forgotten it: the reign of God is God's government set up in the human heart. In this, the human being is a temple, an abode, a place where God can reside, occupy, set up shop, and conduct divine activity throughout the earth. Only when God occupies a heart can it be said that the reign of God has come to earth, starting with Jesus, expanding to a small band of followers, and then into all the earth and in every generation. God's government established in the human heart looks like the fulfillment of prophetic eschatology in Isaiah 2:2-4:

> In the days to come
>> the mountain of the LORD's house
>> will be the highest of the mountains.
>> It will be lifted above the hills;
>>> peoples will stream to it.
> Many nations will go and say,
> "Come, let's go up
>> to the LORD's mountain,
>> to the house of Jacob's God
>>> so that he may teach us his ways
>>> and we may walk in God's paths."
> Instruction will come from Zion;
>> the LORD's word from Jerusalem.
> God will judge between the nations,
>> and settle disputes
>>> of mighty nations.
> Then they will beat
>> their swords into iron plows
>> and their spears into pruning tools.
> Nation will not take up sword
>> against nation;
>> they will no longer learn
>>> how to make war.

The values of God's government are peace, righteousness, love, and justice. When God sets up government, then peace shall reign, and human beings shall beat swords into ploughshares and will study war no more. The reign of God in the human heart is fulfillment of the prophetic hope of political freedom, moral perfection, and earthly (material) happiness to the whole human race.

The reign of God that Jesus announced is inaugurated in Jesus' coming in the here and now and yet will be only fully realized upon the second coming of Jesus. Jesus' deeds, words, life, and death inaugurated the reign of God, and Christians everywhere work and watch for the second coming of Jesus Christ, which will be the final consummation of the reign of God. Jesus left the church to continue the work of the reign of God until the final consummation. One interpretation of what the reign of God looks like in the modern time is Martin Luther King, Jr.'s concept of the "Beloved Community."

King and the Beloved Community

Early in his public ministry, King used the term *Beloved Community* consciously. For example, in 1957, writing in the newsletter of the newly formed Southern Christian Leadership Conference, he described the purpose and goal of that organization as fostering the "beloved community" in America.[12] After about 1960, King no longer used the term *Beloved Community* specifically, though the meaning, concepts, values, and priorities of the Beloved Community flowed in his speeches, writings, and actions for the rest of his life.

There have been astute definitions of King's concept of the Beloved Community by several noted scholars. Kenneth Smith and Ira Zepp define the Beloved Community as "a vision of a completely integrated society, a community of love and justice wherein brotherhood would be an actuality in all of social life. . . . Such a community would be the ideal corporate expression of the Christian faith."[13] Commenting that "the central theme of black theology was the hope of freedom and reconciliation into a community of good will," David Bobbitt suggests that "King called this the 'Beloved Community,' saw it as synonymous with the Kingdom of God, and depicted it in his theme of the 'dream.'"[14] What the American public knows as the "I Have a Dream" speech is essentially King's vision of the Beloved Community. Also, the call for a "revolution of values" and the abandonment of American exceptionalism to join a worldwide fellowship of "the sons and daughters of God" is the beloved community.

King's concept of the Beloved Community has four strands. The first strand is the black theology of the black church evidenced in words spoken by Jeremiah Wright, Jr., in chapter 6:

The prophetic tradition of the black church has its roots in Isaiah, the 61st chapter, where God says the prophet is to preach the gospel to the poor and to set at liberty those who are held captive. Liberating the captives also liberates those who are holding them captive. It frees the captive and it frees the captors. It frees the oppressed and it frees the oppressors. The prophetic theology of the black church during the days of chattel slavery was a theology of liberation. It was preached to set free those who were held in bondage, spiritually, psychologically and sometimes physically, and it was practiced to set the slaveholders free from the notion that they could define other human beings or confine a soul set free by the power of the gospel.[15]

Second, King encountered and was heavily influenced by the social gospel message of Walter Rauschenbusch. In the late–nineteenth- and early–twentieth-century religious movements of orthodox American Protestantism, the emphasis was on individual morality and personal redemption. Rauschenbusch believed this individual emphasis ignored the social role and responsibility of religion and called the church to speak against the brutal social conditions caused by rapid industrialization. He perceived an unfolding social crisis in America and mobilized American Christians to work for a more just society for all, especially the urban working class. He taught that the kingdom of God was collective and that the individual is redeemed through participation in a redeemed and moral social order, which he termed the *beloved community.* Rauschenbusch stressed the Old Testament prophets. Their religion was public, in sympathy with the poor and oppressed, and sought the social redemption of the nation.

The third major influence was a major school of theological thought called *personalism.* Boston University, where King did his doctorate, was the center for the study of personalism. Consider this primer on its basic concepts:

The universe is an organic whole, an interacting system of persons with the central and supreme personality being God. All persons are imperfect copies of the Supreme Personality, yet have inherent dignity and worth because they participate in the ultimate reality of God. Thus, the central tenet of personality, the intrinsic value of all human beings.[16]

King embodied the central tenets of personalism in many of his speeches. His most famous articulation of it is in the 1963 "Letter from Birmingham City Jail."

For King, all human beings are related, and life is social; and because all human beings imperfectly partake of the essence of a moral and loving God, everyone has the capacity for moral improvement. Thus, for King and personalism, the goal of human existence is the creation of a loving and moral society, the Beloved Community.

The last influence on King was the cultural myth of America and the American Dream as noted in a commencement address in 1961 at Lincoln University entitled "The American Dream."

King's concept of the Beloved Community merged the hope and freedom of the black church, the social gospel, the theology of personalism, and the cultural myth of America and the American Dream. King was able, as Bobbit says, "to translate the African American religious themes of freedom and reconciliation into the community, and the concept of God as a personal loving being who values the dignity and worth of each human being, into terms acceptable to white Protestant America. These themes culminated in King's vision of the redeemed and integrated society, which he called the "Beloved Community."[17]

Lessons for Our Struggle

Our purpose is to cause an uprising of ordinary American citizens, particularly pastors, their congregations, and all people of goodwill, to remove the economic interpretation of the American Dream from its stranglehold on the nation. The exaggerated view of capitalistic economic striving as part of the cultural myth of America has come fundamentally to define the person as a consumer. This value, this consumerist definition of human personality, has led to the demise of the American Dream for the overwhelming vast majority of American citizens. Jesus' concept of the reign of God and King's concept of the

Beloved Community define human personality from a healthier and more healing biblical perspective and offer two critical values that must guide our struggle to reclaim the American Dream: (1) the ritual of benefit to the collective rather than exclusively to the individual(s), and (2) the dignity and worth of human personality.

The Ritual of Benefit to the Collective
Rather Than Exclusively to the Individual(s)

The reign of God and the Beloved Community are illustrative of the power of the ritual of benefit to the collective rather than exclusively to the individual. The reign of God is the fulfillment of the prophetic hope of political freedom, moral perfection, and earthly (material) happiness *for the whole human race.* The emphasis is on the benefit for the whole human race rather than for any one group, people, or nation, such that none can choose and justify with myth who gets the ritual of benefit and who does not. As Rauschenbusch states, the kingdom of God is collective, and *the individual is redeemed through participation in a redeemed and moral social order*—not based on the individual accumulation of wealth, power, property, and success.

Individualism emerged in the late nineteenth and early twentieth centuries with the rise of the consumerist ethos. In consumerist culture, the individual and his or her wants, wishes, and needs remain supreme to the exclusion of the collective, even to the point that in a time of cataclysmic national crisis, when individual citizens collectively have the means to bail the financial system out from the credit freeze threatening the entire world economy, the American citizenry is not even asked or challenged to participate. We chose to let foreign sources fund our financial crisis, and the word *sacrifice* has virtually disappeared from the American vocabulary. Except for the military and their families, sacrifice on behalf of the nation is a foreign concept. The result of the consumerist definition of human personality is cultural expressions of patriotism, in which military families sacrifice and "pay the ultimate price" and everyone else gets to go to Disneyland. The malady of our time is not just that we do not have jobs or have a stagnant economy, but that without a reworking of our national values to the benefit of the collective, then we will not be able to sustain the unleashing

144

of creative energies—enterprise, speculation, community building, personal initiative, industry, confidence, idealism, and hope—unsurpassed by any other modern nation. We will continue to justify to ourselves operation in the negative side of the twin dynamics of empire.

The Dignity and Worth of Human Personality

The second value that we must carry forth is the dignity and worth of human personality. We are all connected and injustice and poverty anywhere is injustice and poverty everywhere. Consumerist capitalism defines human beings as producers/consumers and diminishes the worth of human personality. When people are defined as consumers rather than human beings first, then human value is based upon what a person can consume. Once consumerist capitalism operates at the level of cultural myth, the consumer diminishes his or her own value and worth and defines himself or herself based upon what he or she can or cannot consume. The consumerist definition of human personality is the struggle and competition of the Esau and Jacob narrative. In a world in which resources and privileges are vulnerable, Jacob sought to be a producer, secure the ritual of benefit for himself, and by trickery reduce Esau to the role of consumer. The result of the consumerist definition of human personality is violence, genocide, racism, and so on, the negative side of the twin dynamics of empire, in which the ritual of benefit accrues to select individuals, groups, people, or nations and others are excluded with convenient justifications.

We must adopt the value of the dignity and worth of human personality and reject consumerism and its associated warrants that provide a spiritual framework and intellectual rationalization for consumerism, including (1) the claims of advertising that commodities have the power to transform the consumer into a more desirable person, (2) the kind of religion in which the world is basically like a shopping mall or Disneyland, or a good place where poverty, injustice, and inequities are only in the mind, and (3) claims that the good and happy life is to consume and therefore the purpose of life is to consume.

The human being must first be defined as a human being, and only incidentally as a consumer. When a human being is defined as a human being, we respect the dignity and worth of human personality, which means that every person has a right to education for their brains, food for their tables, medicine for their bodies, purposeful employment for their heads and hands, and hope for their hearts.

To consider practical insights that will help us reclaim the American Dream, we must gauge the need for reclamation, not only in America, but also across the globe. As we begin our movement to spread the Beloved Community, we must move with all deliberate speed because the consumerist culture of the cultural myth of America is going global and going fast.

The Global Spread of the American Dream

Although it took one whole century to construct the consumer in Western industrial countries, it has taken a decade in the rest of the world. On the heels of the collapse of global communism, capitalism has achieved a new level of strength and world influence. According to Robbins, recent studies show that 1.7 billion people, or 27 percent of the world's population, can be counted as members of the consumer society.[18] William Leach comments that consumerist culture

> appears to have a nearly unchallenged hold over every aspect of American life, from politics to culture, so much so that the United States looks like a fashion bazaar to much of the rest of the world. For some Americans, the continued power of consumerism has led to further degradation of what it means to be an American or of what America is all about. For others, this evolution has only enhanced the country's appeal, making it appear more than ever an Emerald City, a feast, a department store to which everyone is invited and entitled. Just as cities in the United States once operated as generators of consumer desire for internal markets, today America functions similarly on a global scale.[19]

This phenomenon by which people around the world want to emulate consumer capitalism represents what Joseph Nye calls "soft power." Many global countries, following the allure of Hollywood movies and U.S. news and television programming, imitate American lifestyles and values. The same tools that constructed the consumer in America are at work around the globe, especially in China and India: advertising, credit and debt, and the power of positive thinking. The effect of these trends has mirrored the United States: consumer spending has grown supermarkets and chain stores at the expense of mom-and-pop stores. Protests against big-box operators have become widespread across Asia.

The work of the Beloved Community must apply not only to America, but wherever capitalism consumerist culture is found. Let us now construct the citizen-activist.

CHAPTER TEN

THE REIGN
OF GOD

The American victory in the soft war creates the desire of the citizens of the world to become American, with its values, wealth and security umbrella. However, it is impossible for America to grant the American dream to all people who dream it, either in the U.S. or abroad. The danger of creating a desire that cannot be satisfied—whether desire for a certain product or a certain civilization—is the backlash that will follow: waves of protest and dissatisfaction that will translate into a wish to return to one's own history.
—Francesco Sisci

This book's purpose is to cause an uprising of ordinary American citizens, particularly pastors, their congregations, and all people of goodwill, to reclaim the American Dream from its exclusively economic stranglehold on the nation. The challenge is to redevelop America without the negative side of the twin dynamics of American empire, that is, without the exploitation or domination of subjected people. This America will look more like what Martin Luther King, Jr., called the Beloved Community, modeled after Jesus' inauguration of the reign of God. There are two critical values of the Beloved Community that guide this reclamation effort: (1) the ritual of benefit to the collective, and (2) the dignity and worth of human personality. The challenge in this final chapter is to give practical insights that will construct citizen-activists who will reclaim the American Dream and move America to the Beloved Community.

The challenge is daunting because it is difficult to convert the vision and values of the Beloved Community into practical reality because to do so one must achieve both a moral and political consensus. If we achieve the moral without the political, the danger is that "a movement based on moral and religious arguments can often get bogged down in zealous moralism, self-righteousness, religious mythology, and spiritual otherworldliness."[1] Conservative writer Willmoore Kendall predicted in 1964 that the civil rights movement would fail to substantially alter the lives of the black masses because of a lack of true political consensus for the change it was seeking.[2] David A. Bobbitt further clarifies the danger of the moral without the political with this comment on King's "I Have a Dream" speech:

> There is a danger in achieving a moral consensus without achieving a true political consensus to go along with it—that is, without having achieved political consensus on the sacrifices involved and the means necessary to realize the new moral order. King's speech gave America an inspiring vision of a new moral order, but it elided the costs and difficulties of achieving racial equality. King cannot be held entirely responsible for the legacy of his speech, or the way Americans have chosen to use his words. King was a preacher who felt his job was to inspire people and give them a better vision of themselves. His "Dream" speech, although idealistic and unrealistic, did that. But America used the speech as a national mantra. The mere invocation of the words and ideas provide us with symbolic purification and transcendence for our failure to achieve racial harmony.[3]

If we are not careful, we will paint the vision of the Beloved Community without consensus on the sacrifices, costs, and difficulties involved and offer to America easy redemption. We must supply to America a transcendent, idealistic vision as moral leaders and a pragmatic, unifying vision as political leaders. My goal in this final chapter, based on the vision of the Beloved Community, is to construct the citizen-activist and offer sociopolitical action in the here and now with realistic alternatives.

When I say *citizen-activist*, I mean ordinary American citizens, particularly pastors, their congregations, and all people of goodwill, who will nonviolently resist the exclusive economic domination of American life. I mean the identification and mobilization of the ordinary person, a moral and political leader willing to sacrifice and to pay the cost and suffer the difficulties necessary to reclaim the American Dream. To construct the citizen-activist, we must look carefully at several kinds of "capital," in which capital is defined as an advantage or an asset. Although we are most familiar with economic capital, there are other advantages or assets that are important in our struggle, such as natural capital, social capital, political capital, leadership capital, and personal capital. The first three—natural, social, and political capital— I evaluate through the excellent work of Richard H. Robbins. Then, I explore leadership capital and personal capital. Following Robbins's lead, at the close of each section on capital, I offer one suggestion for the citizen-activist of realistic alternatives of moral and sociopolitical action and then point the citizen-activist to the discussion guide for further discussion. The suggestions are offered to give the reader a starting place for activism with regard to the Beloved Community and with full acknowledgment of my limited vision.

The Myth of Perpetual Growth

The phrase *constructing the citizen-activist* is borrowed from Richard H. Robbins. Robbins calls for active resistance to the expansion of capitalism in America and around the globe. As part of the cultural myth of America, capitalism participates in the twin dynamics of American empire. Robbins concentrates on helping us understand the violent dynamic of capitalism. His analysis suggests that the root of many global problems, such as hunger, poverty, environmental degradation, and labor and sexual exploitation, is "the central and unarguable tenet of the culture of capitalism: the need and desire for perpetual economic growth . . . the consumption of ever more goods and services."[4] Robbins argues that this desire for perpetual economic growth, though based upon the cultural myth of America, appears natural, but it is quite destructive.

Robbins warns the reader that objecting to the myth of perpetual growth will not win many friends, because the need for economic progress is deeply entrenched in American life. Even as I write this, the public debate is about the 2012 presidential election and the growth of the economy as the single most important issue as to how people will vote. Many pundits invoke the mantra "It's the economy, stupid!" as a reminder of this most essential issue to the electorate based upon the belief that economic growth is a prime indicator of their personal and the nation's well-being. The preeminence of the economy in American life is based on the cultural consensus of perpetual growth that rarely if ever gets challenged according to Robbins.[5]

The cultural assumption is that if there is perpetual growth, then there will be an abundance of employment, money, goods and services, and so on, and if not, then recession at worst, and a decrease in jobs, money, and goods and services at best. It is true that when the economy does not grow, based on what we believe about the myth of perpetual growth, there are dire consequences. Robbins still argues that the assumption of perpetual growth is false because we do not count the true costs of perpetual growth, and because we do not count the true costs, we are only kicking the can down the road to an even greater recession, loss of jobs, money, and goods and services.

The measure of perpetual growth and the nation's well-being is its Gross National Product (GNP), or Gross Domestic Product (GDP) as it is now called. It is the sum total of money spent or invested in goods and services by households, governments, and businesses. Robbins believes the annual increase in GDP is the single most important statistic in our culture and makes the strong claim, that as we promote growth we also are "literally killing the world."

When he says, "literally killing the world," he means that the growth of economic capital can take place only "by converting nonmonetary forms of capital such as natural, political, and social capital into money and economic growth."[6] He argues that what we term *economic growth* involves "spending our savings and counting it as income, and squandering our capital and calling it growth."[7] He then proceeds to define the conversion of natural, political, and social capital into economic and monetary capital.

The Conversion of Natural Capital

We do not often think of the features of the natural world as capital, but the natural world of the environment that human beings and all other living things draw on for their maintenance, sustenance, and survival is natural capital. Much like money in a bank, natural capital can be preserved, conserved, or recklessly spent and depleted. For example, fresh water is part of our natural capital, and whenever we use water we are drawing important capital out of the bank.

If the natural capital of fresh water is used without constraint for economic growth, what kinds of global upheavals will there be when two thirds of the world's population face severe water shortages? What kinds of social disruption will there be in the United States if we deplete our aquifers of fresh water? Water will become more valuable than gold, or anything else on the planet for that matter. It is clear that natural capital is finite and limited, and as we use it up, it increases the conflict between brothers in Esau-Jacob relationships. When we have unchecked economic growth, resource depletion runs ahead of resource restoration.

Another aspect of natural capital is disposal of our toxic waste. In 2007, there were 500 million obsolete computers in the United States, many destined for landfills, incinerators, or hazardous waste sites. Robbins reports that, if everyone threw them out at once, we would have a one-mile high waste mountain of junked computers the size of a football field.[8] Those computers represent 1.2 billion pounds of lead, 2 million pounds of cadmium, 400,000 pounds of mercury, and 1.2 million pounds of hexavalent chromium, to name a few of the toxic substances from which they are made. The cost of cleaning up these substances, for the most part, is not included in the cost of the goods and services and so must be assumed by the general public.

The myth of perpetual growth, with unrestrained depletion of natural capital, ensures war, conflict, and violence in the human family, and actually brings about the very recessions that give rise to the myth of perpetual growth in the first place.

Here are several suggestions that move us beyond the unrestricted conversion of natural capital for the citizen-activist.

- Devise a "garbage index" to reduce to zero the amount of waste that we pour into the environment that is not recyclable.

- Stop counting the consumption of natural resources as income. Consumption, if it is to be called income, must leave intact the resources to produce the same amount next year. We must stop treating natural capital as a free good. For example, the sale and export of lumber must be treated as a sale of a capital asset that not only generates income but also reduces future income and productivity.[9]

The Conversion of Political Capital

Political capital is an important component of the healthy and long-term functioning of any society. Political capital is the extent to which people can signify by a vote how much access they have to decision makers.

At one extreme is the total and obvious lack of political capital for the slave and the other side is a society in which each and every person is involved in collective decision-making. There are many things that convert political capital into monetary capital, but Robbins starts with authoritarian regimes, the application of deadly force, the undermining of democratic institutions, and economic debt. Authoritarian governments are better for converting political capital into money because they can more easily "suppress labor organizing, confiscate property, put down resistance to environmental destruction, offer generous tax benefits to investors, and cut back on social and education programs, all actions that in the short term encourage economic growth."[10]

It is interesting that in societies with low levels of political rights, an expansion of (democratic) rights stimulates economic growth. However, once a moderate amount of democracy has been attained, further expansion reduces growth because citizens become more interested in social programs and income redistribution, neither of which is conducive to the uninhibited accumulation of monetary wealth.

In order to manage the expectations of the populace, limits on democracy become necessary to ensure uninhibited accumulation of monetary capital, because democracy ensures demands for rituals of benefit to the collective.

Conversion of political capital into monetary capital is also fostered by the concentration of immense power in the hands of global corporations. For example, of the world's one hundred largest economies, half of them belong to corporations. The sales of Mitsubishi Trading Corporation are larger than the GDP of Indonesia, a country with the world's fourth largest population. Recently, American news media reported that Apple Inc. had more cash on hand than the U.S. government.[11] The balance sheet of the U.S. government revealed $73.8 billion of operating cash while Apple Inc. had $76.8 billion on hand. Corporations accumulate and exercise vast amounts of economic and political power in the best interests of their shareholders.

In this period of great recession and anemic slow recovery, as the unemployment rate hovers at 9 percent, when one out of four homes is underwater, and when the middle class and the poor experience story after story of closed plants, withdrawn resources, layoffs, and downsizings, it does not escape notice that jobs and capital flow to cheaper labor markets as corporate profits are at an all-time high. Corporations are sitting on piles of cash that could be reinvested to help the economy, but corporations act to enhance the bottom-line profit to shareholder benefit. The result has been to heighten the consistent belief in America that corporations have too much influence:

> In September 2000, Business Week magazine released a Business Week/Harris Poll which showed that between 72 and 82 percent of Americans agree that "Business has gained too much power over too many aspects of American life." In the same poll, 74 percent of Americans agreed with Vice President Al Gore's criticism of "a wide range of large corporations, including big tobacco, big oil, the big polluters, the pharmaceutical companies, the HMOs." And, 74-82 percent agreed that big companies have too much influence over "government policy, politicians, and policy-makers in Washington."[12]

One of the primary ways that corporate power translates political capital into economic capital is through massive donations to elected officials that generate more monetary capital for corporations. It is tacitly acknowledged and understood in our culture that money gains a hearing and buys influence with elected officials. This stems from the 1886 Supreme Court ruling that a corporation is a natural person under the U.S. Constitution and consequently has the same rights and protection extended to persons by the Bill of Rights, including free speech. There is a federal ban on direct contributions from corporations or unions to candidate campaigns or political parties in races for federal offices. But the recent 2010 Supreme Court ruling in the matter of Citizens United versus Federal Election Commission prohibits government from placing limits on independent spending by corporations for political purposes. As a practical matter, many corporations are squeamish about direct political alliances and financial advocacy. The real impact of Citizens United has been to unleash the era of unlimited spending to political action committees (PACs). Ruth Marcus suggests that "the rise of these groups erodes the twin pillars of a functional campaign finance system; limits on the size of contributions and timely information about who is writing the checks."[13] Many fear unlimited contributions that, for all intents and purposes, go directly to the candidate may amount to legalized bribery. Citizens United, in this line of thinking, takes campaign financing reform back to pre-Watergate days.

To give the reader the true sense of PACs and their ability to subvert political capital into monetary capital, consider Republican presidential candidate Newt Gingrich's recent complaint of being "Romney-boated," a reference to the Swift-boat attacks on John Kerry in 2004. Fellow Republican presidential candidate Mitt Romney's super PAC, "Restore Our Future," spent $4 million in ads attacking Gingrich. Apparently, the ads worked, because Gingrich's poll numbers tanked. Let's look at the makeup of "Restore Our Future":

> The committee is run by Carl Forti, political director of Romney's 2008 campaign. Its treasurer is Charles Spies, the Romney 2008 general counsel. Its fundraiser, Steve Roche, headed the Romney 2012 finance team until jumping to the super PAC last summer. And to underscore the flimsiness of the PAC's supposed independence, Romney himself has spoken at "Restore Our Future" events.[14]

Ultimately, the effect of the super PAC is that it allows unlimited negative attack ads on an opponent without a candidate being forced to take responsibility for the messages by stating that they approved the message.[15] Some pundits suggest that Gingrich's complaint is in essence that his super PAC did not have as much money as Romney's super PAC and therefore could not counter the negative ad campaign. In other words, this is the political process in America: whoever has the most money can run the best attack ads.

Romney and Gingrich are not the only ones who have a super PAC. Many other politicians do, including Barack Obama. The super PAC is both a Democratic and Republican phenomenon, and it speaks to the excessive role of monetary capital in our political process. Without significant advocacy for change, we are headed for a future in which more and more political capital will be converted into monetary capital at the expense of democracy and the ritual of benefit to the collective.

Consider these suggestions to move beyond the unlimited conversion of political capital for the citizen-activist:

- End the legal fiction of corporate personhood. The 1886 Supreme Court ruling that granted corportions the same rights as persons changed American history.
- Implement serious political campaign reform to reduce the influence of money on politics.[16]

The Conversion of Social Capital

The concept of social capital is clearly defined by the work of Robert D. Putnam in his important book *Bowling Alone:*

> Social capital refers to connections among individuals—social networks and the norms of reciprocity and trustworthiness that arise from them. In that sense, social capital is closely related to what some have called "civic virtue." The difference is that "social capital" calls attention to the fact that civic virtue is most powerful when embedded in a dense network of reciprocal social relations. A society of many virtuous but isolated individuals is not necessarily rich in social capital.[17]

Putnam documents the measurable decline in social capital over the past century and concludes, "by virtually every conceivable measure, social capital has eroded steadily and sometimes dramatically over the past two generations."[18] Putnam uses bowling as an example: the number of people who bowl has increased in the last twenty years, but the number of people who bowl in leagues has decreased. When people bowl alone, they do not participate in social interaction and civic discussions that might occur in a league environment. Bowling in leagues allows people to improve their lives by building social networks of commonality that help people fulfill individual and community goals. When social capital is strong in a community, people are more likely to serve. They tend to feel that most people can be trusted and most people are honest.

Social capital involves social networks in which a "trust currency" develops to resolve problems and to make decisions collectively. Some argue that technology, such as the rise of social media, has dramatically increased social networks and "trust currency" in the first decade of the twenty-first century. Social capital can also be destructive in the fact that groups such as the Ku Klux Klan used social capital to intimidate, exclude, and commit outright murder.

Putnam attributes the decline in social capital to four factors: (1) slow, steady replacement of a long "civic generation" by a generation of less-involved children and grandchildren, (2) the advent of electronic entertainment, particularly television, (3) time and money pressures on two-career families, and (4) increase of suburban sprawl that creates communities with no centers. Robbins argues that what contributes to the decline of social capital also contributes to economic growth, because through our policies, we have encouraged such things as suburban sprawl, which reduces contact among people and also costs families more time and money. Interestingly, TV is also a culprit, because it exposes families to hours of ads and images that promote the idea that happiness is wrapped up in the things we buy.

Robbins lists three other important ways of squandering social capital for economic growth. First, there is the creation and increase in social inequality. Social inequality breaks down trust currency by creating unnecessary boundaries among people; boundaries increase mistrust and resentment and necessitate the creation of ideologies that attempt to justify social differences as natural differences. Second, economic debt concentrates wealth and power in the hands of a few and further accelerates social inequality. The result of debt is that the great majority of people become indebted to a tiny minority. Debt creates wealth for some and extreme poverty for others, devastating individuals, families, and communities. Robbins notes that as the GDP has risen in the United States, so has economic inequality, the gap between the rich and the poor. Third, the movement of corporations from one country to another in search of profits squanders social capital.

Robbins concludes that based upon the myth of perpetual growth in GDP, many decisions that favor economic growth are made to the detriment of natural, political, or social capital, and the American quality of life diminishes. Our national obsession with greater and greater wealth is like blinders on a race horse. We create a consumption expectation that is well beyond what is reasonably required, and in so doing we miss other vital indicators of the quality of life. Economic factors are important, but the exclusive economic reductionism that functions at the center of the cultural myth of America is detrimental to American life. A nonprofit public policy institute, Redefining Progress, proposes the Genuine Progress Indicator (GPI) in lieu of GDP. The GPI begins with household consumption but adjusts it by adding other things, for example, the value of housework and volunteer work. Then it subtracts the cost of environmental pollution, crime, noise, family breakdown, and so on. The upshot is that the while GNP has risen over the last decades, the GPI has declined.

Consider these policies to build social capital for the citizen activist:[19]

- Encourage people to shop in small local shops run by merchants they know by name rather than mega-shopping malls and large retail chain outlets as well as local farmer's markets rather than chain supermarkets.

- Avoid commercial television and devote free time to community gardens, community choirs, or school boards; become a Big Brother or Big Sister; form a fitness/health group with neighbors; volunteer for youth football, baseball, basketball, and soccer leagues; form a bowling team and league; volunteer to deliver meals.

Leadership Capital

One of my major mentors, the late Edwin H. Friedman, argued that leadership is a resource much like air, water, minerals, and so on. He believed that leadership was more valuable than natural resources because leadership often determines the use or misuse of natural resources. Leadership gives a society, culture, or family distinct advantages in the meeting of challenges, flourishing in their environment and enhancing longevity. Leadership in these terms is an asset or advantage, and we could then define it as capital and comfortably utilize the term *leadership capital.*

One critical aspect of leadership capital is the ability of the leader to articulate and inspire a common vision that unifies diverse followers to meet challenges that usually involve some aspect of shared sacrifice. A vision or cause that calls for shared sacrifice forces followers out of their own individualism and into some common purpose or destiny. Leadership capital is the amount of clarity, decisiveness, creativity, and courage that any leader brings to challenges that a group, family, or culture may confront. Friedman believed that leadership was difficult in this "age of the quick fix," and many leaders suffered from "a failure of nerve." As a result, by and large, leaders are not decisive, creative, clear, or courageous:

> I believe that there exists throughout America today a rampant sabotaging of leaders who try to stand tall amidst the raging anxiety-storms of our time. It is a highly reactive atmosphere pervading all the institutions of our society—a regressive mood that contaminates the decision-making processes of government and corporations at the highest level, and, on the local level, seeps down into the deliberations of neighborhood church, synagogue, hospital, library, and school boards. . . . The more immediate threat to the regeneration, and perhaps survival, of American Civilization is internal, not external. It is our tendency to adapt to its immaturity. To come full circle, this kind of emotional climate can only be dissipated by clear, decisive, well-defined leadership. For whenever a "family" is driven by demand-feeding, what will always be present is a failure of nerve amongst its leaders.[20]

The toxicity of our highly reactive atmosphere creates leaders who function in spin, doublespeak, half-truths, blame, impossible pledges and promises, and whatever drivel the public wants to hear, rather than speak the truth. How else can we explain leaders who will not forthrightly tell the American people hard truths, for example, that the old middle-class jobs in America can be done much more cheaply elsewhere and may not be coming back to America?

We need leadership capital to articulate and inspire a common vision that will unify the nation to meet this middle-class job-loss challenge. But levels of rugged individualism and the breakdown of social and political capital are such that it is highly difficult to articulate a vision to unify the nation. Are we too anxious to allow anyone to lead us to a common destiny or a national purpose? Is the massive "failure of nerve" in our leadership indicative of the massive failure of nerve in the people, and do leaders mirror the character and maturity of the people? What is our national purpose? What is our common destiny? Leadership capital assists us to face these questions and meet our destiny.

Too much of our leadership capital is converted into monetary capital and economic gain for the few. The classic example of leadership capital converted into monetary capital is how leaders misuse leadership capital, run corporations into the ground, and then upon their exit get grand bonuses, while rank-and-file workers get nothing. The parent company of American Airlines filed for Chapter 11 bankruptcy reorganization, and the blame was primarily directed at workers. Management, Wall Street, and news reports suggested that American Airlines' problems began with its well-paid and union-represented employees. Several longtime American employees were quoted as acknowledging higher labor costs than competitors but suggested that just cutting employees' pay and pensions would not solve the airline's problems. To a person, employees interviewed said the problems were far bigger than labor, and "American has suffered for years from weak leadership, poor choices and poorly timed decisions."[21] Cox quotes the employees:

> It wasn't the unions, they say, that put off buying new, fuel-efficient jets. It wasn't rank-and-file employees who made the moves that lost market share to competitors. It wasn't the mechanics who ticked off the Federal Aviation Administration

and caused it to ground hundreds of American's planes for days on end because of improper wiring. They say American's management . . . lacked a clear, coherent strategy and that it fostered a business culture that spent more time on nickel-and-dime tactics than on a broader vision of providing its customers with a consistently high-quality travel experience. They point to what they call a massive, entrenched bureaucracy and way too many middle managers and supervisors.[22]

Cox identifies that a lingering issue for workers was the $100 million in bonuses that executives received after persuading workers to take $1.6 billion a year in pay cuts and other concessions in 2003, to keep the airline out of bankruptcy. American employees concede to being very well paid before 2003 and compared to other workers in society remain well paid. They point out that concessions the unions granted to keep American Airlines out of bankruptcy in 2003 went beyond just a simple wage cut or working a couple of more days each month. For example, indicative of employees' sacrifices, pilots took an across-the-board 23 percent cut in pay. Many were forced to fly different planes, captains were bumped down to first officers, and first officers were bumped to less desirable routes and planes. Management's motto after the brush with bankruptcy in 2003 was "Pull together, win together." "They seemed to be doing that at first," said Christine Daniels, a ten-year Air Force veteran pilot who has been a first officer (co-pilot) at American since 1999.[23] But the goodwill vanished with the management bonuses, which came once the airline was profitable in 2006. American filed for bankruptcy protection November 29, 2011, after failing to reach a new contract with the Allied Pilots Association, its pilots union. But the flight attendants and ground workers don't blame the pilots and suggest that the failure of the company has to do with misuse of leadership capital.

Here are several suggestions to inhibit the conversion of leadership capital to monetary capital:

- Any leader or potential leader who will not forthrightly tell followers that sacrifice is called for is not the right leader. True leaders call the followers to sacrifice and articulate a mission and vision that is worth sacrificing for.

- When a leader talks about shared sacrifice, for example, cutting the deficit or asking employees to take a cut in pay and benefits to save the company, make this comment to every leader: Because sacrifice often means sacrifice for other people and not the leader or the leader's group, please tell me the cuts that affect your district and constituency. Cuts that affect your district and voters are called real sacrifice. Tell me what the executives are willing to give up in bonuses, stock options, salary, and benefits to save the company. Sacrifice has often meant the people at the bottom or someone else's constituency should take cuts, while the people at the top or my district pay lip service to the concept.

Personal Capital

Personal capital is closely related to personal responsibility, when personal responsibility is defined as a person's "response-ability," that is, the ability of a person to maturely respond to the various challenges and circumstances of life. Personal capital is also closely connected with character, when character is defined as a person's moral or ethical quality, and the character of a person gives them advantages to respond to the challenges of life. Personal capital, then, is the inner resources, assets, and advantages of personal responsibility and character that one brings to the challenges and circumstances of life. When personal capital is low, a person is a victim of circumstances, at the effect of life and not able consciously and purposefully to choose his or her own thoughts, feelings, and actions. Victims typically identify themselves based upon attributes of powerlessness, dependency, entitlement, apathy, worry, fear, self-doubt, and the like. The victim lives at the effect of what happens around them and has little personal capital to, in response to the challenges of life, choose and direct life's direction and destiny.

Each of us must exercise our personal capital and choose our response to challenges in the external environment. One huge economic challenge in the external environment was already mentioned: the kind of work that built and sustained the middle class in America can be done much more cheaply elsewhere; and in all probability the old middle-class jobs are not coming back, and therefore, the middle-class lifestyle is threatened for many. Coupled with this huge challenge is another reality that Bill Clinton articulated in a 1996 presidential radio address: "The era of big government is over."[24] This means that while middle-class jobs are shrinking and the middle-class lifestyle is threatened, the government is less in a position to provide a social safety net. Ann McFeathers interprets Clinton's words: "He could not foresee that we would be in the dire straits deficit-wise . . . but he did understand that we cannot sustain unlimited growth in entitlement programs. We do have to take responsibility for ourselves."[25] Her words, "we cannot sustain unlimited growth in entitlement programs" and "we do have to take responsibility for ourselves," struck me at my core in terms of my personal responsibility and character and ignited my personal capital.

The challenge of fewer middle-class jobs forces my personal capital to confront and modify the American cultural myth of ever-increasing consumption of goods and services and live according to principles very different from compulsive spending, ostentatious display, and individual material fulfillment. My values are more in line with frugality, moderation, self-denial, and the spiritual and intellectual values of the Beloved Community, the ritual of benefit to the collective, and the dignity and worth of human personality. I reject the myth that the purpose of life is to consume. I am a human being first and only incidentally a consumer. I reject the belief that products make me a more desirable person and give me a richer, fuller life. I am a citizen-activist of the reign of God, and my goal is the Beloved Community. Therefore, I must cultivate several values to live successfully in the face of the challenges of the shrinking middle class and limits to government entitlement programs.

First, debt is bondage, and the only economic freedom that middle-class and poor people have is freedom from debt. While the rich and the elite have the ability to be "independently wealthy," true independence for the middle class and the poor is the ability to live without debt. I realize that debt is necessary at certain critical junctures in life. I realize that there is good debt such as mortgages, school loans, business loans, and so on, and there is bad debt such as credit cards and payday loans. I realize that debt allows us to innovate, create new products, and, when successful, create new jobs. I advocate and support the responsible use of debt. But after the Great Recession, I watched how banks were bailed out by taxpayers based on "too big to fail," and then those same banks foreclosed on the homes of American citizens who loaned them the money in the first place; how the "sins" of Wall Street and banks were "forgiven" by a generous government and beneficent taxpayers, but the "sins" of average people were and still are being counted against them in foreclosures, court judgments, and ruined credit reports. I determined that the only freedom I can have is to owe no one. I resolved in my heart to get out of debt as fast as I could. I am an apostle of debt-free living.

Second, it is my responsibility to be employable. It is not anyone's responsibility to employ me. One of the saddest sights on the American landscape is to see people beg for employment in order to provide for their families and take care of themselves. James Trunslow Adams warned that we had become a nation of "employees" and that we would have to face the fact that employers operate in their own best interests; and when and if it is not in their best interest to keep workers, they will downsize, restructure, lay off, furlough, and slash salaries and benefits.[26] I determined that I had better learn to operate in my best interest and become resilient and innovative in providing the resources I need. It is my responsibility to retool myself, to develop skills to keep myself employable, to nurture the talent and resources to open my own business, and to cultivate proficiencies that ensure that I am marketable and can compete on the global scale for resources. While emergencies and tragic situations happen to all, and we can never guarantee or predict the future, I cannot sustain a family and a life on government entitlement programs and begging someone for a job.

Third, I believe that it is the responsibility of every citizen-activist to be a philanthropist. While many of us believe that Bill Gates, Warren Buffett, and Oprah Winfrey are philanthropists and the average citizen does not have that kind of capacity, I believe that it is the responsibility of every citizen-activist to be a philanthropist. We are not to live our lives maxed out in credit and debt such that we have no margin to be generous to contribute to our churches, synagogues, and mosques and to endeavors of goodwill in our local community and around the world. For those who believe that only the rich and elite can be philanthropists, meet Oseola McCarty.[27] Oseola McCarty was a black washer woman who gave $150,000 to the University of Southern Mississippi and received the Presidential Citizens Medal in 1995. McCarty's gift astounded everyone, and especially those who believed that they knew her well. The customers who brought their washing and ironing to her modest frame home for more than seventy-five years read like the social register of Hattiesburg, Mississippi. She had done laundry for three generations of some families. It made no difference that she washed clothes for a living; she was a philanthropist because she had a passionate desire to leave something for someone else. Upon giving the gift, she said, "I just want to help somebody's kid go to college." She discovered that it's a lot more fun to choose whom to give your money instead of being forced to give it to those who already have, such as the banks.

In order to further the values of the Beloved Community, the following suggestions are for the citizen-activist, with more discussion located in chapter 10 of the workbook:

- Debt is bondage and the enemy, particularly "bad" debt. Debt should be used only with the guidelines established by personal finance experts such as Dave Ramsey (www.daveramsey.com) and Suze Orman (www.suzeorman.com).

- In order to establish a lifestyle as a philanthropist, live off of 80 percent of what you make; give 10 percent away to church, religious charity, mission work, or a high-quality nonprofit; and save 10 percent to pay cash, build your net worth, and be available for future philanthropic endeavors.

Before we move to the workbook, one final word to the citizen-activist.

EPILOGUE

Encouraging the Citizen-Activist

*And it ought to be remembered that there is nothing more difficult to
take in hand, more perilous to conduct, or more uncertain in its success,
than to take the lead in the introduction of a new order of things.
Because the innovator has for enemies all those who have done well under
the old conditions, and lukewarm defenders in those who may do well under the new.*
—*Niccolò Machiavelli,* The Prince

I am certain that given the omnipresence and seeming omnipotence of the economic interpretation of the American Dream and its consumerist orientation and values, the measures outlined herein seem small and insignificant, on one hand, and daunting, with a high improbability of popular support for change, on the other hand. The goal of the book is to cause an uprising of ordinary American citizens, particularly pastors, their congregations, and all people of goodwill, to reclaim the American Dream. The challenge is to redevelop America without the negative side of the twin dynamics of American empire, that is, without the exploitation or domination of subjected people. This America will look more like what Martin Luther King, Jr., called the "Beloved Community," modeled after Jesus' inauguration of the reign of God. This America will unleash creative energies—enterprise, speculation, community-building, personal initiative, industry, confidence, idealism, and hope. I want to close the book with one final piece of commentary to encourage the citizen-activists.

Our politicians present stale, warmed-over twentieth-century ideas that find difficult traction in this new less U.S.-centric, more knowledge-driven, and more competitive world. Rather than tell the

American people the truth—that we have a crisis of historic proportions that threatens this nation to the core of its ideals—and rally the nation with sacrifice and creative ideas to win and meet the economic and social challenges of the twenty-first century, our best response seems to be theatrics, partisanship, sound bites, and tired twentieth-century economic ideas.

The Republicans are proposing twentieth-century tax cuts for the rich—in effect, "trickle-down" economics. We have had "trickle-up" economics for the last thirty years, as we have watched the largest transfer and uploading of wealth to one class of people in human history, while the wages of workers have stagnated. I have absolutely no confidence that when given tax breaks the wealthy and corporations use the savings to benefit working-class American people. They pay dividends, give bonuses, buy back stock, and execute their investment options around the world. A twenty-first-century idea about tax cuts for the rich and corporations is to restrict the funds gained from tax cuts to investment and job creation in the United States and not funnel them through U.S. companies destined for a foreign location. Big business is all about the global economy and not job creation in America.

Historically, the Democrats have used government apparatus to create jobs. The problem is that to create jobs, the government has to tax, and the more jobs the government creates, the more taxes citizens incur. In the twenty-first century, we cannot tax our way to the 8 million jobs that we need. A big portion of government stimulus money and the Troubled Asset Relief Program (TARP), an asset purchase program enacted by the government during the financial meltdown, might have been better spent to provide money for the small business segment, especially new and expanding businesses in high-growth global industries. Small businesses, not big business or government, create 60 to 70 percent of all jobs. A twenty-first-century idea is to give more money to stimulate small businesses and community banks (not Wall Street–owned banks) with the mandate to loan to black, Hispanic, and rural businesses in some of the most severely depressed areas. Both of these measures would have created jobs in America and not China, India, and Mexico.

We do not have a financial problem in America. We have an idea and innovation problem in leadership that cannot be solved by theatrics, calling one another names, throwing tantrums, giving ultimatums, and demonizing unions, the rich, the government, and government workers. Our problem can only be solved by leaders who want to serve the people, leaders who want to work together toward a common vision to benefit the people, leaders who want to inspire the people to sacrifice based on a future for our children, and leaders who want every American to have a job that can provide education, housing, medicine, and food for their families. Consider the man who robbed a bank and asked for one dollar. After securing the dollar, he sat over to the side and waited for the police to arrest him. He wanted to go to jail so that he could receive health insurance. We deserve better than this.

The Great Recession and its aftermath demonstrates that the American Dream is available only to a few people. It presents the citizen-activist with a unique and precious window of opportunity. Citizen-activists must seize this moment while consistently reminding ourselves that results are up to God. Our job is to protest and dissent on behalf of the Beloved Community at whatever level and place we feel called of God to act. No act of nonviolent resistance is too small or insignificant.

Finally, I remind the citizen-activist of what Senator Robert F. Kennedy said at the University of Cape Town, South Africa, on June 6, 1966, at the height and seemingly limitless intransigence of apartheid:

> Thousands of unknown men and women in Europe resisted the occupation of the Nazis and many died, but all added to the ultimate strength and freedom of their countries. It is from numberless diverse acts of courage such as these that the belief that human history is thus shaped. Each time a man stands up for an ideal, or acts to improve the lot of others, or strikes out against injustice, he sends forth a tiny ripple of hope, and crossing each other from a million different centers of energy and daring, those ripples build a current which can sweep down the mightiest walls of oppression and resistance.[1]

I remind citizen-activists that apartheid in South Africa is now gone!

DISCUSSION GUIDE

1. The American Jeremiad and the Cultural Myth of America

1. What are cultural myths? Why are cultural myths important?

2. Define the European jeremiad. Give an example of scripture that a European jeremiad might use.

3. What is the American jeremiad? Give an example of scripture that an American jeremiad might use. (Hint: see the John Winthrop "A Model of Christian Charity" quotation in chapter 1.)

4. What is the chief difference between the American and the European jeremiad?

5. How does the American jeremiad treat concerns of subjugated groups over access to freedom, liberty, justice, citizenship, economic participation, equality, voting rights, and so on?

6. What is the difference between "unfulfilled values" and "structural flaws" in the American Dream?

7. How is the middle class defined, and what is the connection between the middle class and the American Dream?

8. What is the officially endorsed cultural myth of America that subsequently became the American Dream?

9. What is the secular form of the American jeremiad?

10. What are the three premises and conclusion of the secular American jeremiad?

(a)

(b)

(c)

(d)

11. What is the basic form of the secular jeremiad employed by many politicians?

12. Explain why the 1984 U.S. presidential campaign ad of Republican Party candidate Ronald Reagan, known as "Morning in America," is a secular jeremiad.

13. Define the African American jeremiad.

14. What did a reformist and assimilationist form of protest rhetoric developed by blacks, whites, abolitionists, and progressive reformers call America to do?

15. What did the radical, black nationalist, and separatist tradition outside of the jeremiad believe about America?

16. In summation, what is the American Dream? And what is the cultural myth of America?

2. The Cultural Myth of America

1. Why is it important to consider the perspective of subjugated and dominated people in the discussion of the American Dream?

(a)

(b)

(c)

2. What is the author's definition of *imperialism?*

3. Describe one dynamic of the twin dynamics of American empire according to Bercovitch.

4. Describe the other dynamic of the twin dynamics of American empire according to Bercovitch.

5. How would you define *American exceptionalism?*

6. Bercovitch offers the critical insight "that the jeremiad has always restricted the ritual of consensus to a certain group within the culture." What group does the author suggest had access to the American Dream?

7. What is the access point to the American Dream?

8. What is the acceptable form of American dissent?

9. What are the steps of the cultural myth of America's co-optation of dissent?

10. What part of the cultural myth of America is Paul Robeson arguing against in his exchange with Chairman Francis E. Walter during Robeson's appearance before the House Un-American Activities Committee, June 12, 1956?

11. Why does the author call this chapter a "balanced" perspective on the cultural myth of America?

12. Give an example of dissent that is outside of the American jeremiad.

3. The Fall of the American Dream

1. What are the external factors in the decline of the American Dream?

2. What are the internal factors in the decline of the American Dream?

3. Is the true American Dream a promise of material plenty? If not, what is the true American Dream?

4. When dealing with change, what does Adams say becomes of prime importance?

5. Describe Adams's understanding of the ugly scars left on Americans by three centuries of exploitation and conquest of the continent.

6. Why does Adams say that the definition of the human being as a consumer is destructive?

7. What is wrong with America becoming a "nation of employees"?

8. What do Adams and Warren mean when they say that wealth is a "social product"?

9. What does Adams define as being "inimical" to the American Dream?

10. What does Adams postulate as a solution to "save the American Dream"?

11. Without the development of "greatness" in the individual souls of citizens, to whom will people look to define a satisfying and human existence?

12. What are the implications of this comment by Adams? "Americans must understand that just because a person is born with a particular knack for gathering in vast aggregates of money and power for himself, he may not on that account be the wisest leader to follow nor the best fitted to propound a sane philosophy of life."

13. What must the church do to "save the American Dream?"

Section 2 and 4. Prophetic Reformation: Martin Luther King, Jr., and the Triumphant March to the American Dream

1. Hanson develops a Christian political theology and calls it "prophetic politics." Describe the prophetic political model in your own words.

2. What are the cardinal characteristics of the prophetic model?

(a)

(b)

(c)

(d)

3. Define a radical reformist jeremiad.

4. What four pivotal assumptions did King and the American public agree upon that shaped King's radical reformist jeremiad?

(a)

(b)

(c)

(d)

5. "Our God Is Marching On" gives us three critical lessons for those who engage in prophetic politics. Define each lesson in your own words.

(a) Lesson One:

(b) Lesson Two:

(c) Lesson Three:

6. Why does King call Selma the most honorable moment in American history?

7. Why is "Our God Is Marching On" the most upbeat, hopeful, and optimistic speech of King's discourse?

8. Why does King connect the battle over voting rights in Selma with the cosmic battle of eternal values of good versus evil?

9. What does the author argue is the distinguishing factor for any movement that has God on its side? Do you agree?

5. Prophetic Transformation: Martin Luther King, Jr., and "Beyond Vietnam"

1. What two periods can King's public discourse be divided into? What is the difference between the two periods?

2. Define *radical transformist dissent.*

3. List four differences between King's speeches "Our God Is Marching On" and "Beyond Vietnam":

(a)

(b)

(c)

(d)

4. What does the author mean when he says, "King is operating as a social prophet . . . more in line with the European jeremiad than the American jeremiad"?

5. List the four characteristics of King's movement away from belief in the basic values of the American Dream.

(a)

(b)

(c)

(d)

6. What are the three critical thematic movements of "Beyond Vietnam"?

(a)

(b)

(c)

7. What does King mean when he calls for a "revolution of values"?

8. Many consider King's "Beyond Vietnam" speech a failure. Why does the author believe the speech failed?

(a)

(b)

(c)

9. What three lessons does the author identify as "lessons for our struggle"?

(a)

(b)

(c)

6. Prophetic Transformation: Jeremiah A. Wright, Jr., and the American Dream

1. What was the sound-bite narrative that the media created around Jeremiah A. Wright, Jr.?

2. What tools did the media use to create this narrative?

3. What do Herman and Peterson conclude that the media firestorm around Wright indicates about the cultural myth of America?

4. What did Rabbi Kleinbaum conclude about Wright's sermon "The Day of Jerusalem's Fall"?

5. Why does Wright refuse the patriotic singing of "God Bless America"?

6. What is Afrocentrism or Afrocentricity?

7. Why does Wright believe the jeremiad is a constricting form of social critique?

8. Explain how Wright challenges American exceptionalism.

9. Why does Wright believe that it is possible that the U.S. government lied about inventing the AIDS virus as a means of genocide against people of color?

10. How familiar are Americans with what Kaveny calls, "the importance of the jeremiad . . . in the nation's political and religious history"?

11. Compare Wright's "God damn America" statement to the statement of distinguished Harvard Professor William James.

12. Following Frank Schaeffer, compare Wright's prophetic challenge of America to the words of right-wing white preachers who rail against America's sins from tens of thousands of pulpits.

13. How does Michael Eric Dyson explain Wright's prophetic indictment of America being labeled as treason?

14. What two forms of prophetic indictment that Kaveny lists are found in the prophetic books of the Bible?

15. What does Kaveny mean when she suggests that all prophetic rhetoric has the potential to rip the moral fabric of the community to which it is addressed?

16. What does Kaveny suggest as a "helpful rhetorical stance" for would-be prophets?

17. What does Wright argue is the purpose of the unknown phenomenon of "the prophetic tradition of the black church"?

18. Why did Wright adopt the rhetorical stance of "signifying" in the question-and-answer session at the National Press Club?

19. What are the two critical lessons of the media's co-optation of Wright's prophetic message for our struggle to reclaim the American Dream?

(a)

(b)

7. Barack Obama and the Multicultural American Dream

1. What does Morgan argue that Obama's presidential run forced all Americans to grapple with?

2. According to Morgan, what are the characteristics of the first- and second-generation black immigrant discourse?

(a)

(b)

(c)

(d)

3. Why do black immigrants hold some of the same prejudices about African Americans as working- and middle-class whites do?

4. Though black immigrant discourse has a component of criticism of African Americans, for what reason is there sympathy and solidarity with African Americans as well?

5. According to Morgan, why did many African Americans initially believe that the possibility of an African American president was remote and in the far distant future?

6. Do you agree with Morgan's assessment that Obama is a second-generation black immigrant constructing an African American identity in the twenty-first century?

7. What was the importance of Obama's March 18, 2008, speech entitled "A More Perfect Union"?

8. How does Obama resolve the twin dynamics of American empire?

9. What are the practical steps that African Americans must take to "perfect the Union"?

10. What are the practical steps that white Americans must take to "perfect the Union"?

11. How did Obama attempt to inaugurate a new discussion on race?

12. Explain why many Americans believe that America is a "color-blind society," in which the problems of race and racism no longer exist.

13. What is the summation of Obama's charge that Wright has a "profoundly distorted" view of America?

14. Give one example of a writer taking Obama to task for several points of his arguments in "A More Perfect Union."

Section 3 and 8. The Rise of Capitalist Values

1. According to the author, what response to September 11, 2001, reveals contemporary core values of American life?

2. According to the author, what response to the Great Recession of 2007 reveals contemporary core values of American life?

3. What is the state of American national values in regard to sacrifice given the stranglehold that capitalism has on the American Dream?

4. In order to gain support for war, what must a president do to the identity of the American audience?

5. What are the four characteristics of war rhetoric?

(a)

(b)

(c)

(d)

6. What was King's awesome task in opposing President Johnson's prosecution of the Vietnam War?

7. Explain from King's perspective how the Vietnam War required an abandonment of American exceptionalism.

8. Explain from King's perspective how the Vietnam War was indicative of an overcommitment to capitalism and free-market economy.

9. What are the four characteristics of King's peace rhetoric?

(a)

(b)

(c)

(d)

10. What did King mean by the phrase "sons [and daughters] of the living God"?

11. Why exactly did the American public reject King's call to give up American exceptionalism, that is, to reconfigure American national identity?

12. What is the difference between the Walt Disney World version of Chief Joseph and the Nez Percé and what actually happened?

13. How do Walt Disney and capitalism in general mask the parts of capitalism that are uncomfortable and disturbing, anything that would keep Americans from consuming?

14. According to Robbins, between 1880 and 1930, the American definition of a good and happy life changed to consumerism. How were the universe of the consumer and the consumer itself created?

(a)

(b)

(c)

(d)

15. Robbins argues there was a transformation of spiritual and intellectual values from 1880 to 1930—from thrift, modesty, and moderation to periodic leisure, compulsive spending, ostentatious display, and individual fulfillment. What were the four factors that contributed to this transformation?

(a)

(b)

(c)

(d)

9. The Beloved Community

1. What fundamental dilemma within the human family are we asking Jesus to resolve?

2. Define what Westermann means when he suggests that family is the basic form of human community with brotherly and sisterly love and also the prosecution of conflict based upon the scarcity of resources.

3. How does Jesus resolve the twin dynamics of empire?

4. Define the messianic idea, the transforming act and power of God, often released through the Messiah.

5. What text did Jesus utilize to announce the fulfillment of messianic hopes?

6. How would you define Jesus' concept of the "reign of God"?

7. What are the characteristics or the expressions of the reign of God, that is, the church?

8. What is meant when it is said that the reign of God is "God's government established in the human heart"?

9. What is King's interpretation of the reign of God in the modern time?

10. How do Smith and Zepp define King's concept of the Beloved Community?

11. How is King's "I Have a Dream" speech indicative of his vision of the Beloved Community?

12. How is King's call for the abandonment of American exceptionalism indicative of his sense of the Beloved Community?

13. What are the four strands of King's concept of the Beloved Community?

(a)

(b)

(c)

(d)

14. What did King learn from black theology that influenced King's concept of the Beloved Community?

15. What did King learn from Walter Rauschenbusch that influenced his concept of the Beloved Community?

16. What did King learn from the theological school of personalism that influenced his concept of the Beloved Community?

17. How did the cultural myth of America and the American Dream influence King's concept of the Beloved Community?

18. Based upon your responses to the above questions (14–17), write your own definition of King's concept of the Beloved Community.

19. If we would reclaim the American Dream from its capitalistic stranglehold on the nation, following Jesus' concept of the reign of God and King's concept of the Beloved Community, what two values must guide our struggle?

(a)

(b)

20. Define the "ritual of benefit to the collective" in your own words.

21. Define the "dignity and worth of human personality."

22. Explain the expansion of consumerist culture around the world and therefore the need for the Beloved Community around the globe.

10. The Reign of God

1. In converting the vision and values of the Beloved Community, what is the danger in achieving a moral consensus without achieving a true political consensus to go along with it?

2. What is the author's goal in the final chapter?

3. What is meant by the term *citizen-activist?*

4. Define *capital*, and list the five kinds of "capital" in this final chapter.

(a)

(b)

(c)

(d)

(e)

5. What is the central and unarguable tenet of the culture of capitalism?

6. What is the cultural assumption behind perpetual growth?

7. Why does Robbins argue that the assumption behind perpetual growth is false?

8. What is the measure of perpetual growth? Define *perpetual growth.*

9. What does the author mean when he says perpetual economic growth is "literally killing the world"?

10. Define *natural capital.*

11. What costs do we not count in the price of our computers? And what does it mean to "externalize" those costs?

12. Define *political capital.*

13. Why are authoritarian regimes better at converting political capital into money?

14. How is it that a moderate amount of growth in democracy reduces economic growth?

15. Why do the majority of Americans believe that "business has gained too much power over American life"?

16. What is the real impact of the 2010 Supreme Court ruling in the matter of Citizens United versus Federal Election Commission?

17. Define *social capital.*

18. To what does Putnam attribute the decline in social capital?

(a)

(b)

(c)

19. What are the other three ways that Robbins lists for squandering social capital?

(a)

(b)

(c)

20. What is redefining growth in terms of GPI in lieu of GDP?

21. Define *leadership capital.*

22. Friedman believed that leadership was difficult in this "age of the quick fix," and many leaders suffered from a "failure of nerve." What did Friedman mean?

23. How do we explain leaders who will not forthrightly tell the American public the truth?

24. What do you believe is our national purpose? What is our common destiny?

25. Outline the squandering of leadership capital in the story of the parent company of American Airlines filing for Chapter 11 bankruptcy reorganization.

26. Define *personal capital.*

27. What happens when a person's personal capital is low?

28. What does the fact that the government cannot sustain unlimited growth in entitlement programs have to do with our personal capital?

29. The reality of fewer middle-class jobs may force my personal capital to do what?

30. We must cultivate several values to live successfully in the face of the challenges of the shrinking middle class and limits to government entitlement programs. What are the values?

(a)

(b)

(c)

Epilogue: Encouraging the Citizen-Activist

1. Write in your own words the meaning of the Machiavelli quotation that opens the epilogue.

2. What are the twentieth-century ideas that Republicans are proposing to twenty-first-century challenges?

3. The author suggests that we do not have a financial challenge in America, but that we have an "idea" problem. What does the author mean?

4. What great opportunity does the Great Recession present to the citizen-activist?

5. What is the meaning of Robert F. Kennedy's address in South Africa for our struggle?

NOTES

Introduction

1. James Trunslow Adams, *The Epic of America* (Boston: Little, Brown, and Company, 1931), viii.

2. Fareed Zakaria, "How to Restore the American Dream," *Time*, October 21, 2010, http://www.time.com/time/magazine/article/0,9171,2026916,00.html (accessed November 21, 2011).

3. Chris Taylor, "Is the American Dream Dead?" Reuters, June 23, 2011, http://blogs. reuters.com/reuters-money/2011/06/23/is-the-american-dream-dead/ (accessed December 12, 2011); Suze Orman, "Suze Orman on the 'New' American Dream," March 8, 2011, http://abcnews.go.com/Business/suze-orman-redefines-american-dream-book-money-class/ story?id=13088258 (accessed December 12, 2011); Aaron Task, "President Bill Clinton: Yes, the American Dream Is Under Assault," *Daily Ticker*, September 19, 2011, http:// finance.yahoo.com/blogs/daily-ticker/president-bill-clinton-yes-american-dream-under-assault-231659873.html (accessed December 12, 2011); David Kamp, "Re-thinking the American Dream," *Vanity Fair*, September 2009, http://www.vanityfair.com/culture/ features/2009/04/american-dream200904 (accessed December 12, 2011).

4. Eugene H. Peterson, *The Message Remix: The Bible in Contemporary Language* (Colorado Springs: NavPress, 2003).

1. The American Jeremiad and the Cultural Myth of America

1. Sacvan Bercovitch, *The American Jeremiad* (Madison: University of Wisconsin Press, 1978), xi.

2. Gary Colombo, Robert Cullen, and Bonnie Lisle, "Thinking Critically, Challenging Cultural Myths," in *Rereading America: Cultural Contexts for Critical Thinking and Writing* (Boston: Bedford/St. Martin's, 2001), 3.

3. Bercovitch, *American Jeremiad*, xi.

4. John Winthrop, "A Model of Christian Charity," in *The Puritans,* ed. Perry Miller and Thomas H. Johnson (New York: Harper & Row, 1963), 195–99.

5. Avihu Zakai, *Exile and Kingdom: History and Apocalypse in the Puritan Migration to America* (Cambridge: Cambridge University Press, 1992), 129.

6. Ibid., 130.

7. Bercovitch, *American Jeremiad*, 9.

8. Sacvan Bercovitch, "Investigations of an Americanist," *The Journal of American History* 78, no. 3 (December 1991): 978–79.

9. Ibid., xii.

10. Ibid., xiii.

11. "United States History Special Focus: Antebellum Reform," http://apcentral.college board.com/apc/members/repository/us-history-sf-antebellum-reform.pdf (accessed December 12, 2011).

12. M. Kathleen Kaveny, *Prophetic Discourse in the Public Square*, 2008 Santa Clara Lecture: Santa Clara University, November 11, 2008, 6, http://www.scu.edu/ignatiancenter/events/lectures/upload/w-09_Kaveny_Lecture.pdf (accessed October 17, 2009).

13. Ibid., xiv.

14. David Howard-Pitney, *The African American Jeremiad: Appeals for Justice in America*, rev. and exp. ed. (Philadelphia: Temple University Press, 2005).

15. Ibid., 6.

16. For Lincoln, Roosevelt, and Carter see Ernest G. Bormann, "Fetching Good Out of Evil, a Rhetorical Use of Calamity," *Quarterly Journal of Speech* 63 (April 1977): 130–39; for Reagan see "Ronald Reagan's Economic Jeremiad," *Central States Speech Journal* 37 (Summer 1986): 79–89. For Nixon, see Kurt W. Ritter, "American Political Rhetoric and the Jeremiad Tradition: Presidential Nomination Acceptance Addresses, 1960–1976," *Central States Speech Journal* 31 (Fall 1980): 160. For George W. Bush, see "George W. Bush's Post September 11 Rhetoric of Covenant Renewal: Upholding the Faith of the Greatest Generation," *Quarterly Journal of Speech* 89, no. 4 (November 2003): 293–319. For Barack Obama, see Geneva Smitherman, "It's Been a Long Time Comin, but Our Change Done Come," in *The Speech: Race and Barack Obama's "A More Perfect Union,"* ed. T. Denean Sharpley-Whiting (New York: Bloomsbury, 2009), 184–204.

17. Ritter, "American Political Rhetoric and the Jeremiad Tradition," 160.

18. Wilson Moses, "The Black Jeremiad and American Messianic Traditions," in *Black Messiahs and Uncle Toms: Social and Literary Manipulations of a Religious Myth* (University Park: Pennsylvania State University Press, 1982), 30.

19. The African American jeremiadic tradition begins in written form in 1788, when a free black from Maryland, who used the pen name "Othello," wrote "Essays on Negro Slavery" and adapted the jeremiadic form, warning America of God's judgment for the sin of slavery. Another jeremiadic form that has attracted much attention is the work of David Walker. Though Walker's 1829–30 *Appeal in Four Articles Together with a Preamble to the Coloured Citizens of the World, But in Particular, and Very Expressly, to Those of the United States of America* has received much attention as black nationalist discourse, it was black nationalism in the jeremiadic form (David Walker, *The Appeal* [New York: Hill and Want, 1965]). The *Appeal* was written in direct response to and with the intent of refuting Thomas Jefferson's racial theories of black inferiority and apocalyptic prophecies in *Notes on the State of Virginia* (Thomas Jefferson, *Notes on the State of Virginia* [Chapel Hill: University of North Carolina Press, 1955]). Walker was an American speaking to other Americans, with American interests at heart, and yet he held to a black nationalism that served as motivation and commitment to black demands of American nationality.

20. Moses, "The Black Jeremiad and American Messianic Traditions," 38.

21. Ibid., 32.

22. There were many other examples of blacks utilizing the jeremiad, with and without black nationalism: Benjamin Banneker's letter in 1791; Prince Hall's speech "Charge Delivered to the African Lodge at Menotomy" in 1797; Richard Allen and Absalom Jones's "Address to Those Who Keep Slaves, and Approve the Practice" in 1794; Maria Stewart's "An Address Delivered Before the Afric-American Female Intelligence Society of America"; and Frederick Douglass's "What to the Slave Is the Fourth of July? An Address Delivered in Rochester, New York on 5 July, 1852."

2. The Cultural Myth of America

1. Arnold Rampersad and David Roessel, eds., *The Collected Poems of Langston Hughes* (New York: Alfred A. Knopf, 1994), 289.

2. Sacvan Bercovitch, "Investigations of an Americanist," in *The Journal of American History*, 78, no. 3 (December 1991): 978-79.

3. Ibid.

4. Sacvan Bercovitch, *The American Jeremiad* (Madison: University of Wisconsin Press, 1978) xii–xiii.

5. M. Kathleen Kaveny, *Prophetic Discourse in the Public Square*, 2008 Santa Clara Lecture: Santa Clara University, November 11, 2008, 6, http://www.scu.edu/ignatiancenter/events/lectures/upload/w-09_Kaveny_Lecture.pdf (accessed October 17, 2009).

6. Bercovitch, "Investigations of an Americanist," 160, italics added.

7. Michael Novak, *Choosing Our King: Powerful Symbols in Presidential Politics* (New York: McMillan, 1974), 290.

8. See A. Susan Owen, "Memory, War, and American Identity: 'Saving Private Ryan' as Cinematic Jeremiad," *Critical Studies in Media Communication* 19, no. 3 (September 2002): 274.

9. John M. Murphy, "'A Time of Shame and Sorrow': Robert F. Kennedy and the American Jeremiad," *Quarterly Journal of Speech* 76 (1990): 402.

10. Ibid., 412.

11. Ibid., 404.

12. Ibid., 412.

13. Bercovitch, "Investigations of an Americanist," 983.

14. Ibid., 983–84.

15. Paul Robeson was an All-American football player and recipient of a Phi Beta Kappa key at Rutgers and a law degree at Columbia. He became an internationally acclaimed concert performer and actor as well as a persuasive and committed global political activist and speaker. In 1949, newspapers reported Robeson making public statements that African Americans would not fight in "an imperialist war." In 1950, his passport was revoked. Several years later, Robeson refused to sign an affidavit stating that he was not a Communist and initiated an unsuccessful lawsuit. He was called before the House Un-American Activities Committee to answer questions regarding his passport suit. In 1958, the Supreme Court ruled that a citizen's right to travel could not be taken away without due process, and Robeson's passport was returned.

16. House Committee on Un-American Activities, *Investigation of the Unauthorized Use of United States Passports*, 84th Cong., part 3, June 12, 1956; in *Thirty Years of Treason: Excerpts from Hearings Before the House Committee on Un-American Activities, 1938–68*, ed. Eric Bentley (New York: Viking Press, 1971), 770, http://historymatters.gmu.edu/d/6440 (accessed December 15, 2011).

3. The Fall of the American Dream

1. Sylvia A. Allegretto, "The State of Working America's Wealth, 2011," Economic Policy Institute, briefing paper #292 (March 23, 2011), http://epi.3cdn.net/2a7ccb3e9e618f0bbc_3nm6idnax.pdf (accessed December 15, 2011).

2. James Trunslow Adams, *The Epic of America* (Boston: Little, Brown, and Company, 1932), 404.

3. Ibid., 402, 405–6.

4. Ibid., 407.

5. Ibid., 407–8.

6. Ibid., 408.

7. Ibid., 409.

8. Ibid., 410.

9. Madison, "There Is Nobody in This Country Who Got Rich on Their Own," Hotsheet, CBS News, http://www.cbsnews.com/8301-503544_162-20110042-503544.html (accessed April 12, 2012).

10. Adams, *Epic of America*, 413–14.

11. Ibid., 414.

12. Frederick Douglass, "If There Is No Struggle, There Is No Progress" (1857), http://www.blackpast.org/?q=1857-frederick-douglass-if-there-no-struggle-there-no-progress (accessed April 12, 2012).

13. Adams, *Epic of America*, 415.

14. Ibid.

15. Ibid.

16. Ibid., 416.

Section Two: Prophetic Politics and the American Dream

1. Paul D. Hanson, "Prophetic and Apocalyptic Politics," in *The Last Things: Biblical and Theological Perspectives on Eschatology*, ed. Carl E. Braaten and Robert W. Jensen (Grand Rapids, MI: Eerdmans Publishing Company, 2002), 52–53.

2. Ibid., 53.

3. Ibid., 56.

4. Prophetic Reformation: Martin Luther King, Jr., and the Triumphant March to the American Dream

1. "Address to First Montgomery Improvement Association (MIA) Mass Meeting, at Holt Street Baptist Church," in *A Call to Conscience: The Landmark Speeches of Martin Luther King, Jr.*, ed. Clayborne Carson and Kris Shepard (New York: Warner Books, 2001), 1–12.

2. Martin Luther King, Jr., "Our God Is Marching On," *The Papers of Martin Luther King, Jr.*, http://www.stanford.edu/group/King/publications/speeches/Our_God_is_marching_on.html (accessed April 7, 2007). See also the written version published in *A Call to Conscience: The Landmark Speeches of Martin Luther King, Jr.*, 119–32. Taylor Branch, *At Canaan's Edge: America in the King Years 1965–68* (New York: Simon & Schuster, 2006), 169, raises cautions about the text of "Our God Is Marching On" in the 1986 sanctioned anthology, *A Testament of Hope: The Essential Writings of Martin Luther King, Jr.* Branch comments that it is difficult to establish a reliable text of this speech in general: "The preserved record of King's speech would be messier than his hastily thrown-together text, reflecting an era in upheaval. Passages were adjusted or skipped. What lasted in print was not what he said. What lasted in memory was not what he wrote in advance." Some of the errors and abridgements appeared first in excerpts compiled

overnight by the *New York Times*. Branch establishes a reliable text by transcribing two different versions of recordings of the original speech. The scholarly consensus is that the text produced by The Papers of Martin Luther King, Jr. Project is the most reliable text to date.

3. Ibid.

4. Ibid.

5. Ibid.

6. Ibid., 3.

7. Ibid.

8. Ibid., 4.

9. Ibid.

10. Ibid., 2.

11. C. Vann Woodward, *The Strange Career of Jim Crow* (New York: Oxford University Press, 2001).

12. In a series of speeches in 1964 and 1965, Lyndon Baines Johnson popularized the idea of the "Great Society." See David Zarefsky, "The Great Society as a Rhetorical Proposition," *The Quarterly Journal of Speech* 65 (1979): 364–78. King is borrowing the phrase from Johnson. It is interesting to note that James Trunslow Adams also uses the phrase. See Adams, *Epic of America*, 411.

13. Langston Hughes, "Let America Be America Again," *The Collected Poems of Langston Hughes*, ed. Arnold Rampersad (New York: Alfred A. Knopf, 1994), 189–91.

5. Prophetic Transformation: Martin Luther King, Jr., and "Beyond Vietnam"

1. Martin Luther King, Jr., "Beyond Vietnam," http://www.stanford.edu/group/king/speeches/pub/Beyond_Vietnam.htm (accessed October 26, 2009).

2. Ibid.

3. Ibid., 9.

4. Ibid.

5. Ibid.

6. Ibid., 4.

7. Ibid., 3.

8. James Russell Lowell, "The Present Crisis," http://www.bartleby.com/102/128.html (accessed April 12, 2012).

9. King, "Beyond Vietnam," 11.

10. Ibid., 1.

11. Ibid.

12. Ibid., 4.

13. Ibid., 5.

14. Ibid., 6.

15. Ibid., 3.

16. Ibid., 7.

17. Ibid.

18. Ibid., 8.

19. Ibid., 9.

20. Ibid., 8.

21. Ibid.

22. Ibid., 9.

23. Ibid., 11.

24. Ibid.

25. Ibid., 10.

26. Ibid.

27. Ibid.

28. Ibid., 11.

29. *Washington Post,* April 6, 1967.

30. *New York Times,* "Dr. King's Error," April 7, 1967, sec. 1.

31. "Dr. King's Disservice to His Cause," *Life* 62, April 21, 1967, 4.

32. Henry E. Darby and Margaret N. Rowley, "King on Vietnam and Beyond," *Phylon,* 47, no. 1 (1986): 43–50.

33. *New York Times,* "NAACP Decries Stand of Dr. King on Vietnam," April 11, 1967.

34. Carl T. Rowan, editorial, *Washington Evening Star,* April 6, 1967. Rowan critiqued the Riverside speech in coordination with President Johnson's White House (see David J. Garrow, *Bearing the Cross: Martin Luther King, Jr. and the Southern Christian Leadership Conference,* [New York: William Morrow and Company, 1986], 554–5). Also see Carl T. Rowan, "The Consequences of Decision," in *Martin Luther King, Jr.: A Profile,* ed. C. Eric Lincoln (New York: Hill and Wang, 1979), 213.

35. Adam Fairclough, "Martin Luther King, Jr. and the War in Vietnam," *Phylon* 45, no. 1 (1st Qtr., 1984): 30.

36. Branch, *At Canaan's Edge,* 594–95.

37. Rowan, "Consequences of Decision," 213.

38. Charles D. Brennan, *Hearings on . . . the Assassination of Martin Luther King, Jr., VI.* (Washington, DC: House Select Committee on Assassinations, 1978), 296–346.

39. Garrow, *Bearing the Cross,* 555.

40. Fairclough, "Martin Luther King, Jr.," 38.

41. "With but One Voice," *The Nation* (April 24, 1967): 515–16.

42. "King Speaks for Peace" *Christian Century* 84 (April 19, 1967): 492–93.

43. Robert L. Ivie, "Metaphor and the Rhetorical Invention of Cold War 'Idealists,'" in *Readings in Rhetorical Criticism,* ed. Carl R. Burgchardt (Pennsylvania: Strata Publishing, 2005), 317–34.

44. King, "Beyond Vietnam," 9.

45. M. Kathleen Kaveny, *Prophetic Discourse in the Public Square,* 2008 Santa Clara Lecture: Santa Clara University, November 11, 2008, http://www.scu.edu/ignatiancenter/events/lectures/upload/w-09_Kaveny_Lecture.pdf (accessed October 17, 2009), 6.

46. Ibid.

6. Prophetic Transformation: Jeremiah A. Wright, Jr., and the American Dream

1. Brian Ross and Rehab E-Buri, "Obama's Pastor: God Damn America, U.S. to Blame for 9/11," *Good Morning America*, ABC Television, March 13, 2008.

2. Edward S. Herman and David Peterson, "Jeremiah Wright in the Propaganda System," *Monthly Review* (September 2008), 1, http://www.monthlyreview.org/080901herman-peterson.php (accessed December 8, 2008).

3. Ibid., 3.

4. M. Kathleen Kaveny, *Prophetic Discourse in the Public Square*, 17.

5. Herman and Peterson, "Jeremiah Wright in the Propaganda System," 1.

6. Ibid., 3.

7. The ninety-six–day period was from Wednesday, February 27, through Sunday, June 1. Factiva database searches were carried out under the "All Sources" category on June 2. Actual parameters were: [first name w/2 last name] AND [first name w/2 last name].

8. Herman and Peterson, "Jeremiah Wright in the Propaganda System," 5.

9. Ibid., 9.

10. Martha Simmons and Frank A. Thomas, *9.11.01: African American Leaders Respond to an American Tragedy* (Valley Forge: Judson Press, 2001), 81–93.

11. Arthur S. Leonard, "A Different Perspective on Rev. Jeremiah Wright," Leonard Link, http://newyorklawschool.typepad.com/leonardlink/2008/10/a-different-per.html (accessed December 8, 2008). Rabbi Sharon Kleinbaum is senior rabbi of Congregational Beit Simchat in New York City.

12. From "The Day of Jerusalem's Fall" (September 16, 2001), Brian Ross, Avni Patel, and Rehab El-Buri, "Rev. Wright Beyond the Bite; See His Context for Yourself," April 24, 2008, http://abcnews.go.com/Blotter/story?id=4718613&page=1 (accessed December 8, 2008).

13. From "Confusing God and Government" (April 13, 2003), ibid.

14. Molefe Kete Asante, *Afrocentricity* (Trenton, NJ: African World Press, 1988), and *An Afrocentric Manifesto: Towards an African Renaissance* (Boston: Polity Press Publishers, 2007); James H. Cone, *A Black Theology of Liberation*, 2nd ed. (Maryknoll, NY: Orbis Press, 1986), and *Risks of Faith: The Emergence of a Black Theology of Liberation 1968–1998* (Boston: Beacon Press, 1999).

15. In an interview with me, Wright attributed his African-centered thinking, theology, and worldview to his work as a historian of religions as a student of Charles Long and his immersion in the works of Cheikh Anta Diop, William Leo Hansberry, Chancellor Williams, John Henrik Clarke, Geneva Smitherman, and John Lovell. The subject of Wright's master's thesis at Howard University under John Lovell was the African-centered perspective of being agents and not subjects of their own or European history. Wright attributes his support of liberation theology to the writings of James Cone and Gayraud Wilmore, and the teachings of Chuck Long, whom Wright studied under at the University of Chicago for six years.

16. Barack Obama, "A More Perfect Union," March 18, 2008, http://www.americanrhetoric.com/speeches/barackobamaperfectunion.htm (accessed December 9, 2008).

17. Transcript of Jeremiah Wright, Jr., at the National Press Club, http://www.chicagotribune.com/news/politics/chi-wrighttranscript-04282008,0,3113697.story?page=1 (accessed April 12, 2012).

18. See "The Origins of the HIV Virus by Reverend Jeremiah Wright, Jr.," http://www.youtube.com/watch?v=1WAPmMYvvWs&NR=1 (accessed December 13, 2008).

19. See James H. Jones, *Bad Blood: The Tuskegee Syphilis Experiment*, new ed. (New York: The Free Press, 1993); "The Tuskegee Syphilis Experiment," Tuskegee University, http://www. tuskegee.edu/Global/Story.asp?s=1207586 (accessed December 13, 2008).

20. Kaveny, *Prophetic Discourse in the Public Square*, 18.

21. William James to F. C. S. Shiller, 6, August 1902, William James Papers, Houghton Library, Harvard Univerity.

22. Richard E. Welch, *Response to Imperialism* (Chapel Hill, N.C.: University of North Carolina Press), 122.

23. Herman and Peterson, "Jeremiah Wright in the Propaganda System," 7.

24. Frank Schaeffer, "Obama's Minister Committed 'Treason' but When My Father Said the Same Thing He Was a Republican Hero," http://www.huffingtonpost.com/frank-schaeffer/ obamas-minister-committe_b_91774.html (accessed March 20, 2009).

25. Ibid.

26. Kaveny, *Prophetic Discourse in the Public Square*, 3.

27. Professor and author Michael Eric Dyson compares MLK to Jeremiah Wright, http:// newsguru.newsvine.com/_news/2008/04/04/1410426-professor-author-michael-eric-dyson-compares-mlk-to-jeremiah-wright (accessed December 15, 2011).

28. Kaveny, *Prophetic Discourse in the Public Square*, 19.

29. Ibid., 3.

30. Ibid., 10.

31. Transcript of Jeremiah Wright, Jr., at the National Press Club.

32. Ibid.

33. Ibid.

34. The Bill Moyers Journal, http://www.pbs.org/moyers/journal/04252008/profile.html (accessed April 28, 2009).

35. "Transcript of Jeremiah Wright's Speech to the NAACP," CNNPolitics.com, http:// www.cnn.com/2008/POLITICS/04/28/wright.transcript/index.html (accessed April 28, 2009).

36. Amy Sullivan Washington, "Jeremiah Wright Goes to War," *Time*, April 28, 2008, http://www.time.com/time/politics/article/0,8599,1735662,00.html (accessed March 20, 2009).

37. "The Dozens," http://en.wikipedia.org/wiki/Playing_the_dozens (accessed March 20, 2009).

38. Transcript of Jeremiah Wright, Jr., at the National Press Club.

39. Thurman Garner and Carolyn Calloway-Thomas, "African American Orality: Expanding Rhetoric," in *Understanding African American Rhetoric: Classical Origins to Contemporary Innovations*, ed. Ronald L. Jackson II and Elaine B. Richardson (New York: Routledge, 2003), 53.

40. Roger. D. Abrahams, *Talking Black* (Rowley, MA: Newbury House, 1976); Thomas Kochman, "Toward an Ethnography of Black American Speech Behavior," in *Rappin' and Stylin' Out: Communication in Urban America,* ed. Thomas Kochman (Urbana: University of Illinois Press, 1972); Henry. L. Gates, *The Signifying Monkey* (New York: Oxford University Press, 1988); Geneva Smitherman, *Talkin and Testifyin: The Language of Black America* (New York: Holt, Rinehart, and Winston, 1977); Claudia Mitchell-Kernan, "Signifiying as a Form of Verbal Art," in *Mother Wit from the Laughing Barrel: Readings in the Interpretation of Afro-American Folklore*, ed. Alan Dundes (Englewood Cliffs, NJ: Prentice-Hall, 1973); T. Garner, "Understanding Oral Rhetorical Prac-

tices in African American Cultural Relationships," in *Towards Achieving Maat*, ed. V. J. Duncan (Dubuque, IA: Kendall/Hunt Publishing, 1998).

41. D. G. Myers, "Signifying Nothing," *The New Criterion* (February 1990), 61-64, http://www-english.tamu.edu/pers/fac/myers/signifying.html (accessed on March 20, 2009).

42. In an interview with the author, Wright pointed out that the mood shift had to do with the obvious and total "dissing" of his scholarly presentation and the continued apparent "dissing" of the black religious experience. Wright suggested that his presentation was the first of several powerful and professional presentations, "The Prophetic Witness of the Black Church," given at a three-day conference sponsored by the Samuel DeWitt Proctor Conference for pastors. Following Wright's presentation that morning, there were papers presented by John W. Kinney, the Dean of the School of Theology at the Samuel DeWitt Proctor School of Theology at Virginia Union University and President of the Association of Theological Schools; Katie Cannon, one of the country's leading womanist theologians and professor at Union Theological Seminary; and Dwight Hopkins, Professor of Theology at the University of Chicago Divinity School—papers that echoed the presentation made by Wright in his opening presentation. The professional papers were followed by two days of panel discussion held by professors and graduate students at the Howard University School of Divinity.

43. Washington, "Jeremiah Wright Goes to War."

44. David A. Frank and Mark Lawrence McPhail, "Barack Obama's Address to the 2004 Democratic National Convention: Trauma, Compromise, Consilence, and the (Im)possibility of Racial Reconciliation," *Rhetoric and Public Affairs* 8, no. 4 (2005): 586.

7. Barack Obama and the Multicultural American Dream

1. Joan Morgan, "Black Like Barack," in *The Speech: Race and Barack Obama's "A More Perfect Union,"* ed. T. Denean Sharpley-Whiting (New York: Bloomsbury, 2009), 55–68.

2. Ibid., 59.

3. Ibid.

4. Ibid., 60.

5. Ibid., 64.

6. Ibid., 64–65.

7. Ibid., 67.

8. Ibid.

9. Ibid.

10. Ibid.

11. Ibid.

12. Barack Obama, "On My Faith and My Church," *Huffington Post*, March 14, 2008, http://www.huffingtonpost.com/barack-obama/on-my-faith-and-my-church_b_91623.html (accessed December 8, 2008).

13. Obama, "A More Perfect Union," 2.

14. Lincoln-Douglass Debate, Last Joint Debate at Alton, Illinois, October 15, 1858, http://www.bartleby.com/251/72.html (accessed December 15, 2008).

15. Obama, "A More Perfect Union," 3.

16. Ibid.

17. Ibid., 2.

18. Ibid.

19. Ibid.

20. Ibid.

21. Ibid., 3.

22. Ibid., 4.

23. Ibid.

24. Alice Randall, "Barack in the Dirty, Dirty South," in *The Speech: Race and Barack Obama's "A More Perfect Union,"* 205–33.

25. Ibid., 221.

26. Obama, "A More Perfect Union," 3.

27. Ibid., 5.

28. Ibid., 6.

29. Ibid., 5.

30. Ibid., 6.

31. Ibid., 6–7.

32. Ibid., 7.

33. Ibid., 8.

34. Ibid.

35. Ibid.

36. Ibid.

37. Ibid.

38. Ibid., 9.

39. Ibid.

40. Ibid.

41. Ibid., 9–10.

42. Ibid., 10.

43. Ibid.

44. Ibid.

45. Jonathan Alter, "Ringing the Bell," *The Daily Beast*, March 17, 2008, http://www.thedailybeast.com/newsweek/2008/03/17/ringing-the-bell.html (accessed April 13, 2012).

46. Tim Rutten, "Obama's Lincoln Moment," *LA Times*, March 19, 2008, http://www.latimes.com/news/opinion/la-oe-rutten19mar19,0,5754610.column (accessed December 15, 2008).

47. Hendrik Hertzberg, "Obama Wins," *The New Yorker*, November 17, 2008, http://www.newyorker.com/talk/comment/2008/11/17/081117taco_talk_hertzberg (accessed December 15, 2008).

48. Charles Krauthammer, "The Speech: A Brilliant Fraud," *The Washington Post*, April 4, 2008.

49. Evan Thomas and the Staff of *Newsweek, A Long Time Coming: The Inspiring, Combative 2008 Campaign and the Historic Election of Barack Obama* (New York: Public Affairs Books, 2009), 73–74.

50. Smitherman, "It's Been a Long Time Comin,'" 186.

51. Ibid.,185.

52. Ibid.

53. Adam Mansbach, "The Audacity of Post-Racism," in *The Speech: Race and Barack Obama's "A More Perfect Union,"* 74.

54. Ibid., 83.

Section Three: The Beloved Community

1. "Congress Looks to Shield Economy," CNN, September 15, 2011, http://articles.cnn.com/2001-09-15/us/rec.congress.terror_1_consumer-confidence-capital-gains-tax-minority-leader-dick-gephardt?_s=PM:US (accessed December 23, 2011).

2. Andrew J. Bacevich, "He Told Us to Go Shopping. Now the Bill Is Due," *Washington Post*, October 5, 2008, http://www.washingtonpost.com/wp-dyn/content/article/2008/10/03/AR2008100301977.html (accessed December 22, 2011).

3. Ibid.

4. "Late 2000 Financial Crisis," http://en.wikipedia.org/wiki/Late-2000s_financial_crisis (accessed December 22, 2011).

5. The Constitution Club, "Hope Bonds," http://constitutionclub.org/2009/02/11/hope-bonds/ (accessed December 22, 2011).

6. James Jasinski, "Time, Space and Generic Reconstitution: Martin Luther King's 'A Time to Break Silence' as Radical Jeremiad," in *Public Address and Moral Judgment: Critical Studies in Ethical Tensions*, ed. Trevor Parry Giles (East Lansing: Michigan State University Press, 2009), 97–125.

7. Ibid., 6.

8. The Rise of Capitalist Values

1. "'Chief Joseph' Hin-mah-too-yah-lat-kekt (1840–1904)," New Perspectives on the West, http://www.pbs.org/weta/thewest/people/a_c/chiefjoseph.htm (accessed December 22, 2011).

2. Stephen M. Fjellman, *Vinyl Leaves: Walt Disney World and America* (Boulder, CO: Westview Press, 1992), 104.

3. Richard H. Robbins, *Global Problems and the Culture of Capitalism*, 5th ed. (Upper Saddle River, NJ: Prentice Hall, 2010), 26-27.

4. Ibid., 14.

5. Ibid., 15.

6. Ibid., 19.

7. Ibid., 20.

8. Sylvia A. Allegretto, "The State of Working America's Wealth, 2011," Economic Policy Institute, March 23, 2011, Briefing Paper, http://epi.3cdn.net/2a7ccb3e9e618f0bbc_3nm6idnax.pdf (accessed December 22, 2011).

9. Robbins, *Global Problems and the Culture of Capitalism*, 38.

9. The Beloved Community

1. See chapter 1, pp. 3–4.

2. Claus Westermann, *Genesis 12–36: A Continental Commentary* (Minneapolis: Fortress Press, 1995), 419.

3. Ibid., 23.

4. Ibid., 24.

5. Ibid., 417.

6. Ibid., 418.

7. C. H. Dodd, *The Parables of the Kingdom* (New York: Charles Scribner's Sons, 1961), 29.

8. Henning Graf Reventlow, "The Eschatologization of the Prophetic Books: A Comparative Study," in *Eschatology in the Bible and in Jewish and Christian Tradition*, ed. Henning Graf Reventlow (England: Sheffield Academic Press, 1997), 170.

9. Ibid.

10. Ibid., 171.

11. Yair Hoffman, "Eschatology in the Book of Jeremiah," in *Eschatology in the Bible and in Jewish and Christian Tradition*, 75.

12. Southern Christian Leadership Conference (SCLC) pamphlet, ca. 1960 http://nationalhumanitiescenter.org/pds/maai3/protest/text2/thisissclc.pdf (accessed April 14, 2012).

13. Kenneth L. Smith and Ira G. Zepp, Jr., "Martin Luther King's Vision of the Beloved Community," *Christian Century* (April 3, 1974): 361-63.

14. David A. Bobbitt, *The Rhetoric of Redemption: Kenneth Burke's Redemption Drama and Martin Luther King, Jr.'s "I Have a Dream" Speech* (New York: Rowman & Littlefield Publishers, 2004), 12.

15. Transcript of Jeremiah Wright, Jr., at the National Press Club on April 28, 2008.

16. Bobbitt, *Rhetoric of Redemption*, 13.

17. Ibid., 16.

18. Robbins, *Global Problems and the Culture of Capitalism*, 30.

19. William Leach, *Land of Desire: Merchants, Power, and the Rise of a New American Culture* (New York: Pantheon, 1993), 388.

10. The Reign of God

1. David A. Bobbitt, *The Rhetoric of Redemption: Kenneth Burke's Redemption Drama and Martin Luther King, Jr.'s "I Have a Dream" Speech* (New York: Rowman & Littlefield Publishers, Inc., 2004), 113.

2. Willmoore Kendall, "The Civil Rights Movement and the Coming Constitutional Crisis," http://www.mmisi.org/ir/01_02/kendall.pdf (accessed April 15, 2012). See also Willmoore Kendall, "The Civil Rights Movement and the Coming Constitutional Crisis," *The Intercollegiate Review* 1 (1965): 66.

3. David A. Bobbitt, *The Rhetoric of Redemption: Kenneth Burke's Redemption Drama and Martin Luther King, Jr.'s "I Have a Dream" Speech* (New York: Rowman & Littlefield Publishers, 2004), 114.

4. Robbins, *Global Problems and the Culture of Capitalism*, 335.

5. Ibid.

6. Ibid.

7. Ibid.

8. Ibid.

9. Both suggestions are from ibid., 346.

10. Ibid., 340.

11. Brandon Griggs, "Apple Has More Cash Than the U.S. Government," CNN, July 29, 2011, http://articles.cnn.com/2011-07-29/tech/apple.cash.government_1_ceo-jobs-apple-cash-balance?_s=PM:TECH (accessed January 4, 2012).

12. Sarah Anderson and John Cavanagh, "Top 200: The Rise of Corporate Global Power," Institute for Policy Studies, December 4, 2000, http://corpwatch.org/article.php?id=377 (accessed January 4, 2012).

13. Ruth Marcus, "Super PAC Is Logical Citizens United Result," *Commercial Appeal,* January 4, 2012, A5.

14. Ibid.

15. Ibid.

16. Suggestions are from Robbins, *Global Problems and the Culture of Capitalism*, 346–47.

17. Robert D. Putnam, *Bowling Alone* (New York: Simon & Schuster, 2001), 19.

18. Ibid., 287.

19. I recommend "100 Things You Can Do to Build Social Capital," http://www.bettertogethernh.org/bluepic.pdf (accessed January 11, 2011), and "150 Things You Can Do to Build Social Capital," http://www.bettertogether.org/150ways.htm (accessed January 11, 2011). For a more scholarly discussion, see "A Comprehensive Resource on Social Capital and Its Research," http://www.socialcapitalresearch.com/building.html (accessed January 11, 2012).

20. Edwin H. Friedman, *A Failure of Nerve: Leadership in the Age of the Quick Fix*, ed. Edward W. Beal and Margart M. Treadwell (New York: Seabury Books, 2007), 1.

21. Bob Cox, "Workers at Bankrupt American Airlines Say Do Not Blame Us: Wall Street Tied Bankruptcy to Labor Cost, but American's Top Brass Made Own Mistakes," January 5, 2012, http://www.commercialappeal.com/news/2012/jan/05/airline-workers-say-do-not-blame-us/ (accessed January 6, 2012).

22. Ibid.

23. Ibid.

24. CNN Transcript of President Clinton's Radio Address, January 27, 1996, http://www.cnn.com/US/9601/budget/01-27/clinton_radio/ (accessed January 10, 2012).

25. Ann McFeathers, "The World Has Changed Forever," http://www.nashuatelegraph.com/opinionperspectives/917039-263/the-work-world-has-changed-forever.html (accessed April 14, 2012).

26. Adams, *Epic of America*, 409.

27. Oseola McCarty, http://www.answers.com/topic/oseola-mccarty (accessed January 11, 2011).

Epilogue: Encouraging the Citizen-Activist

1. Robert F. Kennedy, "Day of Affirmation," Cape Town University, Cape Town, South Africa, June 6, 1966, http://www.americanrhetoric.com/speeches/rfkcapetown.htm (accessed January 30, 2012).